Other Titles by this Author;

Pools of Unheard Tears

The Cold Hand of Fate

Chaotic Inertia

When the Beat Stops, Then I die

In the Crosshairs of Death

A Bed Full of Vipers

Hell is Best Served Ice Cold

When Death
Smiles Back

By

RM Atkins

3

Preface

As you settle down to sleep at night. Do you ever wonder what tomorrow will bring, or maybe you have sometimes had that feeling that you have been somewhere before. The trouble though, is that no matter how hard you try, you just can't remember when?

Now this story is about a young man called Harry Flynn. He is a 25year old single man that lives in a large rural village called Bedlington out in the countryside. So for convenience he like many others that also live there, travel everyday into the city by train to where he works as an accountant. The only problem that Harry has is that he can never manage to wake up in the morning earlier enough, for him to catch his train to work, or, so he thought!

<u>Chapter One</u>

"Mmm, that was a nice sleep," mumbled Harry, as he stretched and turned over in bed. With his eyelids still reluctant to open, he tried to focus his bleary eyes on his watch, hoping as he did every morning that he had not over slept yet again.

"Hey," smiled Harry, "It's a Friday morning and I've actually managed to wake up on time for once".

Getting out of bed, Harry walked across to the window and pulled open the curtains.

"It looks like we might have some rain later, looking at the clouds hovering above," thought Harry to himself, as he went about his daily morning routine.

Harry, who is five feet ten inches tall with brown hair and eyes, is a twenty five year old who lives in a rural village called Bedlington. Although this is classed as a village, it boasts an arrangement of small shops a bank and a train station. This is very handy as it is a vital life line as a vast majority of the people that live here make the daily commute to the city to work. This journey to the city is a lot easier to do by train as finding a parking space in the city would take up most of his day and cost a fortune over the month just in parking charges!

   This morning began just like any other morning but it would soon turn out to be far from normality. While Harry waited for the bus, he usually liked to watch people as they went this way and that, to and from their own place of work. As the green double-decker bus pulled up at his stop, Harry noticed that something seemed to be different. Today it only had the number (2) on the front of the bus, which was the one he needed but normally there was a destination written on the front as well.
Harry, while sitting on the bus, liked pass the journey time looking out of the window at the

people in the street. From on top of the double decker, it was like looking down at a small colony of ants, all hustling and bustling about. Except this morning there was something different happening, very different indeed. Instead of the people hurrying about their normal business, they were all just standing around with confused looks on their faces. Although this bizarre behaviour puzzled Harry, as it didn't affect him he soon dismissed it from his mind.

But as his bus pulled in outside the front of the small train station, Harry suddenly began to feel a little uneasy.

"What's the matter with me? I've made this journey loads of times. Maybe it's because I'm actually early for a change!" he thought.

As soon as his bus stopped just outside the station entrance. He joined all of the other early morning commuters jostling each other as they made their way through the narrow doorway of the bus that led them onto the pavement. They then all headed towards the display board that is positioned high up on the wall in the centre of the station. This shows travellers which number platform they need to go to and also the time and destination of each train. To his amazement there seemed to be hundreds of people just standing there looking up at the display board!

  After looking around, Harry then asked one of the men who was standing looking up at the board "Why, are there so many people just waiting around, please don't tell me the trains are on strike again?"

The stranger turned slowly towards Harry and said in a confused way, "Why don't you take a good long look up at the notice board and tell me what you see, or, should I say, what you don't see?"

Harry, not wanting to appear rude shrugged his shoulders and looked up towards the notice board and to his amazement it was empty!

Well not completely empty, there were numbers that appeared to be spaced out in no particular order but there were no destinations showing. In fact there were no words of any description to be found on the board at all!

"That's the reason for everyone just standing around, it's because they don't know which platform they have to go to so that they can catch their train?"

"Where's all the station staff?" he asked,

"Surely they must have time tables!"

The man seemed to ignore Harry's question and just shrugged his shoulders and turned back to stare motionless once again back up at the board. Harry looked around and eventually found a uniformed member of staff. His next task was to thread his way through the hoards of people that were just standing gawping up at the empty information boards. Harry finally reached the uniformed member of staff and asked, "Excuse me sir, can you tell me which platform I need to catch my train to the city?"

The man in uniform turned around slowly and half looked at Harry and replied, "I'm sorry sir but I have no idea."

This snide comment really pissed Harry off. Just for once he had managed to get up early for his journey to work and this arsehole couldn't be bothered to answer a simple question "What do you mean you have no idea, you do work here don't you?" snapped back Harry in disgust.

Harry's cutting comment to the man however seemed to have no effect on him in the slightest. Then without a second glance, the man reached into his tunic pocket and took out a book. He then passed it across to Harry and said calmly,
"Well here's my timetable book, would you like to take a look for yourself, sir?"
Harry took hold of the book and with a loud sigh of disgust opened it up, then, he tried to make sense of what he was seeing.
"I don't understand it, where are all of the words. All this book has in it are numbers, why does it not have any words?" he asked.

Then Harry felt a hand lay gently on his shoulder and he turned around and saw that it was the man who had just given him the timetable book.

"Take a good look around you sir and tell me what you see, or, should I say, don't see!" said the man holding out his other arm and pointing at display boards and to the kiosks that sold papers and magazines!

Harry turned slowly around, not knowing what he was supposed to be looking for.

"Do you notice anything unusual?" asked the man in a calm sounding voice.

Harry looked all around and then after a few moments he realised that wherever he looked, there were pictures but no words. All of the advertising boards were empty there were no newspapers, books, magazines, anywhere that had any words in them!

"I don't know what's happening," said the man, "but it appears that all of the words have just disappeared?"

"But this will mean that everything in the world will shut down, because nobody will be able to function without any words!" said Harry aloud.

After standing for a while looking around at all the confused faces on the other commuters.

Harry suddenly decided that he was not just going to stand there like all the other sheep. That was when he decided to turn around to walk back out of the station. It was as he began to turn, he spotted a large group of men all wearing what looked like army camouflage gear, entering the station. One of the men was using a loud hailer to speak to everyone telling them that there had been a lorry crash just outside the village. The lorry had been carrying toxic material and the crash had resulted in a leak of the material into the air. So for their own safety they have to go with them to be checked to see if any of them have been contaminated. When the man stopped speaking, the men dressed as soldiers, proceeded to try and herd everyone into a tight group.

This action along with what the man had just told them, made a lot of the people nervous and some of them tried to break away from the group. As they began to move away from the other people, calls were heard for them to stop and return to the others. This had the desired effect on a few of the people and they moved back into line. Half a dozen though refused to comply, and with calls from them, clearly saying that they needed to get home to make sure that their families was safe. All of them though were quickly brought heavily down to the ground, after being hit individually with fifty thousand volts from several taser guns. Their screams of agony reverberated around the entire station concourse, adding the feeling of terror to the already frightened commuters.

"If you stop trying to escape, then we will stop the pain!" shouted the man with the megaphone.

This unprovoked action onto those already scared people instilled a strong feeling of rebellion in some of the men that were being held captive. They tried to rush some of the army personnel; this action however, forced the rest of the camouflaged men to produce automatic weapons. They then pointed them at the group, forcing everyone back into the tight group.

It was amongst all this mayhem that Harry managed to slip unseen away from the group and made his way down the stairs to one of the platforms. Unfortunately for Harry, one of the army personnel spotted the top of his head as it disappeared down the stairs.

"Hey you stop!" shouted a man's voice loudly.

"Sir, someone's trying to escape onto the platform."

Harry ran down the steps, taking two at a time. All the time from the concourse area, he could hear shouting. Once he was on the platform, he then had yet another problem, where was he going to able to hide?

The loud voices were getting closer every second and he knew that time was not going to be on his side. Then just as several of the armed men began their descent of the stairs, Harry took the only opportunity available to him. Whilst at the edge of the platform and with seconds to spare, Harry leapt off the platform, landing alongside the railway tracks.

"Now what?" thought Harry in a blind panic? "Shit, I know one of these three rails is electrified, but which one?"

Then as he heard the angry voices along with the pounding feet of the men running down the stairs, he instinctively jumped over the rails, ducked down out of sight and crawled underneath the platforms overhang.

Overhead, Harry could hear the men searching behind all the doors looking for him. Their frustration at not being able to locate him was obvious; from the tone of the bad language they were all using.

"He must have jumped onto the line and legged it!" said one of the men, as they stood closer to the edge of the platform for a better look. "Do you want some of us to follow sir?"

Harry who was by now sitting almost directly beneath where the men were standing, could hear what they were saying and was shaking his head as if to try and influence their decision. Just then, there was a loud whoosh sound and Harry had to brace his hands against the concrete roof to prevent himself, being sucked out onto the railway tracks.

An express train was passing through the station at high speed. This action alone could have been enough to suck Harry out of his hiding place, towards the train and certain death. On the platform however, they army personnel also had a fright when the train sped by them with only inches separating them. They had all been looking in the wrong direction when the express approached the station. They too had to jump back from the edge of the platform to prevent being sucked into its path.

The train disappeared as fast as it had arrived, Harry felt drained and partly traumatised by the whole episode. While still shaking from the shock, he had to remember that only inches above him were the enemy. So for the moment, breathing slowly and concentrating on his every action was going to be the order of the day.

"Oh fuck him," said one of the men. "If the train didn't get him, then one of our patrols will.

Let's get back to the others and report in shall we?"

With that, Harry heard the clumping of heavy boots moving away and running back up the stairs. He decided to wait a little while and make sure that those men had all left the platform before he made his move. Then slowly he crawled out of his hidey hole and took a long look both ways along the railway tracks to make sure that they were clear, in case he moved his body into the path of another train.

With the track for the moment clear of trains, Harry moved from hiding and peeped to look onto the platform. When he saw that there were no people anywhere near, he took another look for any trains before jumping up from the tracks back onto the platform.

After dusting himself down, Harry moved towards the stairs and listened for the sound of voices. After listening for a short while, he began the climb back up the stairs towards the stations concourse area. When he was a couple of steps from the top Harry stopped and lay down flat so that he could observe the goings on, hopefully without being seen himself. There in front of him but on the far side of the station, stood a group of people that were now surrounded by armed army personnel. When he noticed that everyone was facing the other way, he crept in a stoop position off the stairs towards an old kiosk, that would have normally sold newspapers to the passing commuters.

  Harry reached the side door of the kiosk and opened it up and slipped inside. Then as if in one complete movement, he crawled under the counter and hid behind piles of magazines and held his breath as the sound of booted feet passed within inches of where he was hiding. He managed to find a hole in the wooden frontage of the kiosk and watched as everyone inside the station was rounded up and forced out of the station. By now the group were all silent as they moved towards the station entrance. Minutes later when the station concourse was clear of people, Harry heard the sound of several powerful sounding diesel engines rev into life.

Then a short time later, he heard them all begin to move away from the front of the station. Harry remained where he was until he could no longer hear the sound of the engines. Then after a good look around through the hole in the wood and seeing nobody about, Harry edged from his hidey-hole and nervously popped his head above the kiosks counter for a better look around. This was now a very eerie place to be, never had he been in this place when it had been totally empty!

"What the fucks going on?" said Harry to himself as he constantly looked all around.

"Why are the army holding us hostage? Oh shit, are they our army or do they belong to another country?"

Slowly, Harry moved from his hiding place and stood for the first time in the centre of the concourse, wondering what he should do next?

As he walked towards the front of the station he was still feeling a little bewildered and confused.

"Where have all the words gone and why have the army come to this place. If the phone lines

go down how will people be able to communicate with each other, there will be no letters, e-mails.
No-one will be able to send or receive orders or even bills!" thought Harry, "although the thought of having no bills would be nice. Maybe, if I go back home then I could get my car out of the garage and drive away from here and tell someone. I think I know how to drive to different places without having to rely on any road signs or maps!"

   Outside the station, the streets were now an eerie place to be, and he felt alone and very vulnerable. Less than an hour earlier, Harry had happily travelled to the station on a bus along with other people heading for the station. Now, the pavements were empty, there were no people moving about. The roads and streets were now totally devoid of any traffic. It was as if he had somehow gone through a time warp. The only difference being, he knew that this was real and very frightening.

"If only I can make it back home without getting caught, then I can try to go and get some help," thought Harry as he looked around in case he was being watched.

Harry made sure that he kept out of the daylight as best he could and edged his way from shop doorway to shop doorway. However, behind every shop window, the premise was totally devoid of people. This village that he loved appeared to have become a ghost town as there was no signs of life to be seen anywhere. It took him over an hour to travel the relatively short distance back to his home. On the odd occasion, Harry would have to throw himself behind some bushes and hide when he heard heavy lorry engines approaching.

Once he was finally back home, he had to take time to rest. Even though the distance to his home wasn't that bad, the concentration needed to stay out of danger had totally drained him. Soon he felt refreshed enough and began to make preparations for his long drive from his

village to the city, which was about forty miles
away, or so he believes!

———————

Chapter two

His car, which was his pride and joy, was in
fact a 1972 year old mini that he was trying to
do up. Although there were patches of rust on
the wings and bonnet. It didn't matter to Harry,
as this was his very first car and it was his pride
and joy!
Harry put the keys into the car's ignition and
gave them a turn. It had been a while since his
pride and joy had been driven and as the engine
cranked over and over, he crossed his fingers.
Finally after some persuasion the little car gave a
cough and a splutter then roared into life. With
the engine now ticking over on the car's manual
choke, Harry made sure that his petrol gauge
showed that he had enough fuel for the journey.
Instinctively he reached into the glove box and
took out a road map to assist him on the journey.
It was only after opening it up, did Harry

discover that on here too there were no words only numbers!

"That's ok," said Harry out loud to himself,

"most of the roads that he needed only had numbers on them anyway."

Then after refolding the map, he put the car into gear and set off. While moving slowly down the road he began to wonder about what he might find on his route to the city. He knew that he had to keep clear of those army men. It wasn't long before Harry approached the final corner that he knew would take him out of town and towards the city.

Suddenly he had to brake hard because there in front of him positioned in the middle of the road was a large blue sign. It had no words on it, just a large white arrow!

This made Harry wonder to himself, why would anyone put a sign in the middle of the road if there were no road works. Now he was in a bit of a dilemma, does he ignore the sign and proceed on his journey to the city, or does he follow the direction that the arrow in front of him seemed to be pointing. Finally it was his curiosity that got the better of him and he decided to follow the arrow to see where it would lead him. For the next few minutes at each road junction he came across, he found even more signs with arrows on them.

It was as if he was being sent around in some kind of circle but instead of annoying him, it just left him feeling more curious by the minute. With thoughts of getting help slipping further and further to the back of his mind he kept following the signs hoping to find out what was going on.

Eventually, while driving down yet another road he came across a large metal gate that was spread across the road, blocking it completely!

"That's funny?" thought Harry, "I have never seen that before!"

He stopped his car and was just going to get out and investigate, when he saw two men dressed in different camouflage clothing and armed with guns coming towards him!

For a brief second he froze and then as they drew closer he began to feel more than a little scared and his stomach began to knot up. When one of the men gestured to him to get out of his car and follow them, Harry began to panic and his mind started racing in all directions. Then in a flash he remembered something that he had seen in a film once. Not wanting to anger the two men who were holding guns, Harry opened his window a little and shouted to the men that his driver door was sticking and could one of them come over and help him to open it.

The two men spoke quietly to each other then one of them slung his gun across his back and came over to the mini's driver's door. As he reached down to open it, Harry, in turn, quickly reached down below the steering wheel and as soon as he felt the ignition key in his fingers, he turned it. When the two-armed men heard the mini's engine suddenly roar into life, for a split second they both seemed a little shocked. Seizing this opportunity, Harry quickly slammed his car into reverse gear and pressed down hard with his right foot on the car's accelerator. As his car began to move backwards at speed, the little cars engine screamed in protest as it propelled them backwards. Harry watched out the corner of his eye as the men both lifted their guns towards him, took aim at his car and fired!

Bang, bang!

  "Fucking hell, they are shooting at me?" shouted Harry out loud.
He ducked down hoping to avoid being shot and quickly reversed his car around one bend in the road then into another side road. As soon as he was out of sight of the men, he quickly turned the car around and engaged first gear. Then with his foot pressed hard down on the car's accelerator he sped away!
Every road junction that he later came to there were more signs with arrows and even more armed men blocking his escape route. It seemed that they were waiting for him to arrive at each road junction.

"The bastards must be talking over their radios about me!" shouted Harry out loud to himself.

With his heart thumping, Harry didn't stop driving until he was clear of the town and far out in the countryside. As soon as he spotted an open gateway leading into a farmer's field, he grasped the opportunity and quickly drove his car through it. He kept driving in the field until he was sure that he could not be seen from the gateway. Then he parked his mini out of sight behind a thick hedgerow and turned his engine off. Then he quietly opened the car door and slid out of the car and onto the grassy floor looking all around in case anyone could see him. When he was sure that he was safe, he gave out a big sigh.

With his head in his hands he muttered softly,
  "What, the hell is going on in this place, are we at war and nobody has told us, or worse, have we already been invaded?"

Now Harry, like most boys when they're growing up, dreamt about being a spy or a secret agent like James Bond, fighting all the bad guys. This though was no dream and as he looked at the fresh bullet holes in his old but faithful mini. He realised that playing secret agents and escaping from people with guns, were totally different in real life and very, very, frightening!

After a few minutes Harry regained his thoughts and decided that he must find a safe place to hide out, maybe until its dark. Deciding that it would be far too dangerous driving on the road in daylight, Harry got back into his mini then carefully drove his car from field to field looking for somewhere safer to hide. Finally away in the distance he spotted a small wooded area that sat on the top of a hillside and he headed off towards it. Once there he was able to hide his car out of sight but more importantly, now he was in a good position to keep watch and see anyone who was approaching him.

From time to time Harry would see army type vehicles pass by his hiding place, but who's were they?

———————

Chapter Three

After what seemed an eternity, Harry thought about how he could get someone to help him escape from the area.

"Maybe the Police could help me!" thought Harry, as he fumbled in his trouser pockets. "Oh shit, where the hell's my phone?"

After a recheck of all his pockets, the realisation that he must have dropped it inside his car suddenly struck him. Now this gave Harry yet another dilemma, does he try and retrieve his phone from his car risking being seen by one of the many passing army vehicles. Or does he reject that idea and stay where he is. After weighing up the pros and cons, Harry decided that doing nothing was futile. Hence, the only other option was for him to return back to where he had left his little car and hope for the best. So from his vantage position, Harry once more scanned all around him looking for anything that could suggest any unwanted approaching company. Then with the coast clear, he took a deep breath and broke from his cover and edged his way back to where he had left the mini. Each step that he made was now more calculated than ever before. Every few paces, Harry would stop suddenly and pan all around him looking for any movement. Finally he made it back to the relative safety of his car.

Dropping onto the ground alongside the mini, Harry leant against the driver's door and caught his breath.

"Right then, let's find that mobile before anyone spots me," said Harry under his breath. He slowly stood up and in a crouching position, carefully opened the door. Then while leaning into the car, he began to search for his phone.

"Bloody hell, I never thought that there was this much rubbish in the car," he muttered to himself.

Then he spotted it on the floor half hidden by one of his floor mats. "Ah, there you are you little bastard, how did you ever manage to get down there?"

It was as Harry reached across to pick it up, that was when he noticed something out of the corner of his eye.

"Hang on a minute," said Harry. "Where the fuck's the keys gone to that I'd left in the ignition?"

"Are you looking for these?" said a man's deep voice from behind him.

Harry froze with fear when he heard that sound, he was now beginning to panic. Was the man standing behind him friendly or not unfortunately, he was now too afraid to even take a look?

Then he heard a sound that raised the fear level even higher. From behind him there came a loud "click!"

That sound alone made Harry quiver with fear. The only other time that he had heard such a sound, was earlier that day at the gated road. It had been there that the two armed guards had both made the exact same clicking sound when they cocked their automatic weapons, prior to firing them at him.

"Right sir," said the man standing behind Harry. "What I want you to do now, is to stand up and turn around slowly to face me is that understood?"
Harry, hearing the man's instructions, did not reply, instead he nodded his head showing that he had heard and understood what he had to do. As he slowly moved his hands to prop himself against the passenger seat, Harry noticed a wheel brace that had been wedged between the passenger seat and the handbrake. In one slow but flowing action, he grasped the heavy metal wheel brace in his right hand and proceeded to edge slowly backwards out of the car's interior. He took great care to shield it with his body from the man until he had the opportunity to use it.

"Right", shouted the man in a rough voice, "I want you to turn around and face me."

Harry took a deep breath and quickly spun round. As he did so, his right arm shot outwards. A loud dull clunk sound rang out as the man was struck on the side of the head by the heavy metal bar.

Harry froze as his eyes and the man's for an instant stared deep into one another. Harry then struck him again with all his strength on the head. The final blow had the desired effect and after emitting a loud groan, the man collapsed unceremoniously to the ground.

All Harry could do was stand there and stare at the man that now had a stream of blood trickling from his head wounds and onto the grass, forming a deep red pool of blood.

"Oh bollocks, what have I done?" said Harry shaking his head as he returned back to reality. With the man who was dressed in camouflage now lying motionless at his feet, he reached down placed his fingers onto the side of the man's neck trying to locate a pulse.

"Shit, I have no idea what I'm doing but I have seen this sort of thing in films when they try to find out if someone's alive or dead," muttered Harry as he moved his hand away from the man's neck after feeling nothing and picked up the man's gun. He thought for an instant about keeping hold of it in case he came across anymore of the man's colleagues. But after looking again at the weapon in his hands, he soon came to his senses. He realised that for one, they would almost certainly kill him if he were to be armed. Secondly, he had no idea how to even fire such a weapon and he would be more likely to shoot himself if he were to ever to actually pull the trigger!

Harry then moved quickly to the nearby hedge and threw the gun into the middle of it. Then he decided to try and move the body away from the mini with the hope that neither of them would be discovered. At first, Harry tried grabbing hold of the man's wrists hoping to drag him along the ground. Unfortunately, the thought of holding onto a dead person made him feel sick in his stomach. Then he tried grabbing hold of the man's tunic and this time he was successful in dragging the dead weight along the field to a spot where he could eventually roll him into the undergrowth and out of sight.

Harry stood there looking at what he had done and an icy chill ran down the entire length of his body making him shudder. This action though managed to bring him out of his gloom and he then was able to focus back onto his mobile phone.

"I hope that the battery is still charged up." He glanced down at it and saw that it was, then after taking a deep breath he began to dial.

RING, ring, went the phone.

"Hello, who's calling 999," said a female voice, "Which service do you require!"

"Police!" said Harry, "I want to talk to the police!"

"I am trying to connect you sir!"
For a brief second the line began to crackle, then!

"Police, how can I help you?" said a deep male voice.

"Something strange is happening in a village called Bedlington where I live, there are men dressed in army uniforms walking around carrying guns!" said Harry, his voice getting faster and faster.

"Excuse me sir but did you just say that there are men with guns," asked the voice on the phone.

"Yes I did and they even fired at me and my car when I tried to escape from them!"

"Right sir, let me recap the situation, men wearing army uniforms and carrying guns. You have managed to escape from them, you say," repeated the voice on the other end of Harry's phone!

"Now then sir, first of all can I have your name and then the address from where you are calling from," asked the policeman.

Harry gave the policeman his name and where in the countryside that he was now calling from. Then the man on the phone told him to wait where he was and someone would soon be there to assist him.

After hanging up Harry at first felt relieved that someone was now coming to help him. It wasn't long before Harry began to worry about what he had said over the phone to the policeman. The other point that nagged at him was, did I really get put through to the police or were the people who seemed to be in control of his town also controlling the phone lines!

Harry then thought that maybe he would air on the side of caution. He decided to leave his car where it was and look for a different place to hide.

After taking a few minutes to scan the field that he was in, he finally saw the ideal hiding place. This was located in some bushes that were incorporated within a very wide hedge that ran around the field. Harry could still see the trees from where he had called the police from and more importantly the road where any police vehicles would appear from.

"If the police turn up then I can easily call to them from over here!" thought Harry, sitting down on the grass and leaning against the hedge. This had been a very long day and as he looked skywards he could see the sun beginning to set and he knew that before long it would be getting dark. He wouldn't have to wait very long, because in the distance Harry soon heard the sound of an engine and it was coming his way!

"That doesn't sound like a normal police car it's more like the sound of a heavy diesel lorry engine!" thought Harry, sinking down to lie flat on the ground so as not be seen. The engine noise came closer and closer and soon it stopped on the grass below where the trees were.

From his vantage point Harry parted the grass below the hedge so that he could get a better view without being seen. There, not too far in front of him stood a large lorry which had a canvass back on it. Even seeing this Harry didn't feel too worried about the situation. At first nothing happened, the driver and his mate just remained inside the cab of the lorry and appeared to be having a good look around. Then without any warning, the rear flaps of the lorry's canvass back were thrown open and men began jumping out and lining up behind the tailgate of the lorry. Harry, seeing this became very frightened when the people that exited the rear of the lorry were not wearing any type of police uniforms that he had ever seen before. Unfortunately for Harry, these men were all wearing the same type of army camouflage as the man that he had not long ago killed and these too are also carrying guns!

In the distance Harry could just make out the sound of voices and they sounded angry. That was when Harry realised that other men also dressed in camouflage gear had been approaching his place of hiding from a different direction. In an instant he drew his knees up into his chest and lay still even trying to hold his breath.
Then one of the men shouted out for the others to spread out and begin a search of the area.

Maybe it was due to the failing light that he was undetected even when some of the men's feet stood within inches of his own. Harry watched as they began their search, some of them, were now having to use torches to see but luckily for him none of the beams of light were ever aimed in his direction.

Time passed slowly and with the arrival of night also meant the lowering of temperature. Being only dressed in his travelling work clothes, Harry soon began to feel a distinct chill emanating from the ground and into his whole body. Then in the distance Harry heard a shout ring out from the darkness. Although he was unable to make out what had been said, he did overhear a message that was being relayed over one of the men's radio.

"Over here sir, we've have found his car," said a voice over the man's radio.
"Are you sure that it is the missing man's car?" was the reply. "Yes, positive, this car also has some recent bullet holes it!"

"Hmm, it used to have some holes in it but none of them were bullet holes before today. I wonder if they'll discover their dead colleagues, body," thought Harry to himself.

From his position under the hedge, Harry watched as shapes carrying torches moved away from where he was and towards the place where he had left his car. Daring to prop himself up slightly, Harry took a slow look around looking for any sign of the search party. He waited for about ten minutes before moving from under the hedge. Then he slowly stood up so that he could stretch his legs to allow the blood supply to flow through them again. Unfortunately that brought on a very uncomfortable bout of pins and needles that spread from his waist right down to his toes. Harry tapped his feet on the ground to help the blood flow again as quietly as he could he did not to draw any unwanted attention in his direction. When the numbness abated and he could feel his feet properly again Harry decided to make a run for it, (a bad mistake!)

Within seconds of Harry breaking cover, he was spotted by men that had been strategically positioned around the field just in case of such an escape attempt. Hearing the uniformed men running close behind him shouting at him to stop, Harry began to run faster than he had ever run before. This time he knew that it could mean the difference between him living or dying! He seemed to have only been running for a few seconds climbing over thorny hedges and jumping small fences, when he began to hear the sound of a different sounding engine. As he ran, the sound of the engine got closer and closer.

Risking falling over, he took a quick glance over his right shoulder towards the sound of the engine noise. To his amazement the sound he had heard was the sound of helicopter. From the underside of the craft there shone a bright search light and now it was shining directly onto him. Within seconds it was directly overhead and it must have been flying very low because Harry could feel the heat from the powerful search light on the back of his neck.

"STOP RUNNING and LAY DOWN ON THE GROUND," roared a voice through a megaphone that was hanging between the helicopter skis.

Thump, thump, thump, went Harry's heart as he felt the wind pressing on him from the down draft of the helicopter blades that was by now hovering only a few feet above his head!
"Stop running or we will have to open fire on you," repeated the voice.
In a split second Harry would have to decide whether to stop running and give up, or does he continue running and risk being shot!

Chapter four

However, before he was able to come to any decision, fate took over. It was as he was running, mostly in a blind panic, the ground below him suddenly gave way and Harry found himself falling down through the ground and into the darkness of the earth below.
From the chasing helicopter, the pilots watched in disbelief as their escapee suddenly disappeared from their sight down a hole that seemed to appear and just swallow him up. By the time that they had turned the helicopter around, the ground had somehow closed up again leaving no sign for Harry's pursuers to find him!

After falling for what seemed like an eternity, Harry suddenly came to an abrupt halt that knocked all the wind out of him. Now down in a deep hole and in total darkness, Harry lay very still on the ground too afraid to move because of the pain that now seemed to spread throughout his body. Somehow he had managed to hit every rock and stone as he tumbled down the hidden shaft, before landing hard on the ground. He was now in total darkness and his nostrils began to sting as he breathed a mixture of damp earth and decaying stench of rotting grass and foliage.

Harry, after a few minutes, reluctantly decided that he would have to try to move and plucked up the courage. Slowly he tried to move his legs, aiding their movement with the help of his hands. To his amazement there did not appear to be anything broken, he was only battered and bruised. Then slowly standing up, trying not to make any noise, in the darkness he strained his ears hoping to hear something, anything from above. After a short while he could just make out the sound of voices but they appeared to be coming from a long way above him. Although they were too far away for him to understand what they were saying, from the tone of their voices they were not very happy that he had escaped capture. Now Harry had a big dilemma, should he call out to the men above and hope that they rescue him. Or does he say nothing and hope that he can escape from this underground tomb!

"Well, I'm screwed if they rescue and capture me and I'm screwed if they don't," thought Harry, as he sat down on the damp earth to ponder his situation.

Harry decided to wait until the sound of the voices had completely disappeared. Then standing up and using only his hands as a guide, he began to feel above him for the hole in the roof where he'd dropped in through. Soon he managed to locate an opening overhead had began precariously to climb back up the hole. It was a long hard climb and several times Harry lost his footing and slipped the long way back down again, adding even more cuts and grazes to his arms and legs. Finally Harry was too exhausted to attempt another climb and he sat down on the ground for a rest and to get his breath back.

Despair wasn't far from Harry's mind, as he wondered how and if he was ever going to get out again.

"Oh stop whining you useless bastard!" said Harry out loud to himself. If you can't climb up then look for some other way to get out of here!" he shouted and slapped the side of his face hard to shake away the doubt.

This seemed to have the desired effect and it wasn't long before Harry's eyes became better adjusted to the darkness. After using a mixture of feeling the sides of the walls with his hands and using his very limited vision, he found that he could just make out the shape, of what appeared to be a hole of sorts. After reaching inside the hole as far as he could without actually climbing in. He discovered that it appeared to go off to the side, but for how long and to where was going to would be anyone's guess. From what he could see and feel, this opening was roughly a couple of feet wide in diameter and at first he wondered if he might become stuck as he tried to crawl through it. The other thing that now began to worry him and play on his mind, was what sort of animal had made this opening and even more important was it still around!

  With only two options available to him. Harry decided that climbing back up the shaft was no longer feasible. The only remaining option was to try crawling into the hole and hope that it takes him all the way to the surface. Standing up slowly, so that he didn't hit his head onto anything, Harry slowly edged his way into the opening of the tunnel. Progress however was very slow due to the instability of the dirt around him. The only way that he could make any progress, was to bend his legs, dig his toes into the soft earth and then push his body forwards. He would have to then try to press his fingers into the soil to prevent him from sliding back down, while he repeated the process. This action although tediously slow, was the only way he could move forwards in such a confined space.

Then it happened, as he tried to dig the toes of his shoes into the loose soil so as to propel him forward. There suddenly a low rumbling sound could be heard and the ground around him began to tremble. Then without any warning, the roof of the tunnel collapsed bringing lots of loose soil and stones down on top of him.

Luckily, when Harry heard the rumble, he stopped trying to move and instinctively placed his hands over the top of his head for protection. It was this action alone that gave him a chance to survive the cave in. Because, as the dirt dropped down the positioning of his hands and arms created a gap beneath is face. Now it was this gap and this gap alone that was enabling Harry to breathe.

"Oh shit!" shouted out Harry in despair as he tried desperately to move his legs and feet. He was reluctant to move his hands as they were still supporting soil and debris from dropping into the air space around his head. At first this action was unsuccessful resulting in a strong feeling of panic swelling up throughout his entire body. As the feeling of being trapped turned into panic, Harry's body felt like it was swelling up, making it feel as though his body was now completely filling the tunnel.

"Fucking hell, man calm down," said Harry to himself. "If you panic now, then you're finished for sure. Then you'll be buried alive!" shouted Harry, trying hard to move his feet under the weight of the fallen soil but to no avail.

Harry tried very hard to relax and save his strength and limited air supply, but all the time he knew that he was on his own and that nobody else was going to help get him out of this mess!

Time after time Harry tried in vain to free his legs from the soil and by now he could tell from his shortness of breath that the trapped pocket of air was quickly running out. Then in a fit of desperation, Harry decided to remove his hands from above his head and try digging himself out at the front. Although the soil was soft and his hands could easily penetrate through it. His real problem was what to do with it after he had managed to dislodge it. The last thing he needed was to add to the already weighty problem down by his legs.

So he tried to pat the moved soil along the sides of the small tunnel, that way it would not add to his problems. This though took a lot out of Harry and breathing was now very difficult indeed. Then as he was about to give up, his final push with his hands went through the soil and he could feel cold air on his fingertips. This then inspired Harry to stretch forwards as much as he could but this time he tried pushing the soil away from him. To his amazement, a small hole appeared just ahead of him and he could feel cool fresh air on his face for the first time. Harry relaxed his body as he gulped in the fresh air.

Now feeling refreshed, he tried once more to move the soil in front of him. Before very long, he had managed to make the hole wide enough for him to get through. Now his problem was his trapped feet and how to free them?

Harry thought for a short while, all the time taking in mouthfuls of cool air into his lungs. Then Harry reached out with both of his hands and tried to gain some purchase with them onto the outer part of the hole.

As soon as he thought that his grip was strong enough, he made a combined effort of pushing with his feet and at the same time he pulled with all his might with his hands. At first it appeared that nothing was happening, then, slowly, his body began to edge forwards towards the open hole. He repeated the action a further twice and finally, his underground tomb slowly released its death hold on him and he was able to drag himself out of the hole and sit free, out in the open air.

Harry lay on his back on the damp grass and stretched his arms and legs as far as they would go. "God that feels good!" said Harry out loud. It was only then, that he remembered how he got into that hole in the first place and about the men who had been after him. Harry lay still listening intently for any sound of the men nearby, but he heard nothing. Sitting up, he took another look around and was pleased to see nothing out of the ordinary. He gazed skywards at the thousands of bright twinkling stars, that looked like they were somehow attached to a dark expanse of velvet. Then his thoughts quickly returned to more earthly thoughts and before he stood up, Harry took one last look into the hole and said quietly,

"Crikey, to think that I could have died and been buried within less than two feet of freedom."

With that disturbing thought in his head, he gave a shudder and promptly turned away from the hole and moved off cautiously into the darkness.

———————

Chapter five

It was now night time and although there was only half the moon visible, there emitted just enough light for him to make out the hedges and the surrounding hillside.

"I wonder where I am?" he thought, straining his eyes into the darkness.

Then, as his eyes become more accustomed to the half moon lit night, the outline of a hill top could just be made out. This was due to the fact that there seemed to be a faint glow of light coming from behind it.

"I wonder if those are the lights coming from Bedlington?" said Harry to himself and decided to head off in that direction.

As he made his way towards the hill top, he was all the time consciously listening for any sound that might be from those army blokes lying in wait to ambush him as he passed by. It wasn't long before he came across a farmhouse that still had all of its lights on. Harry approached the building with extreme caution. Every couple of steps he would stop and have a good look around him and also listen for the sound of voices. On reaching one of the farmhouse windows, he decided to take a look inside. This was possible due to the fact that none of the curtains had been pulled to and the light was on.

Through the window he could see that the room he was looking into was the kitchen. On the huge wooden table there was still food laid out as if whoever lived here was about to have a meal. Harry then edged further along the building to the next window. This time though as he tried to peer through the window he suddenly heard some voices coming from inside. Hearing this he quickly dropped to the floor and almost froze with fear. When however the voices failed to come any closer to him, he plucked up the courage, then, carefully and quietly brought himself to his feet. He took a deep breath, then raised his head very slowly so as not to attract any unwanted attention from whoever was within and peeped through the window.

  At first he saw nobody in the room, then feeling a little braver he stretched up onto his toes and took a good look around the room. To his delight there were no people at all in the room only a television and it was the sound of voices coming from that he must have been hearing.
Now that he was feeling a bit more confident, he decided to move to the front of the farmhouse and try knocking on the door.

  Maybe the farmer had not come across the men with guns and might even be able to help him to tell the authorities or someone!

Knock, knock!

Harry took a small step back from the door, just in case, but nothing happened and nobody came to the door. Harry tried knocking the door again but yet again there was no response. Then with his hands shaking, he took hold of the door knob and tried turning it.

Click went the lock and the door went ajar.

"Hello," called Harry in not too loud a voice.

"Is there anybody there?" repeated Harry, then a weak smile came to his face.

"Bloody hell, I sound like someone from one of those séance meetings."

With more confidence he pushed the door fully open to make sure that there was no-one standing behind it and walked inside. Moving from room to room he felt both relieved and at the same time very uneasy due to the fact that he could not find anyone at all!

"It's like that saying I keep using. The lights are on but no-one's home?" This though was so unreal.

Eventually he found himself in the kitchen and with his stomach making very loud rumbling noises he took the opportunity to eat up some of the wonderful food that was left lying on the table. After filling his stomach, with wholesome food, plenty of water and taking the liberty of using their toilet, he left the farmhouse and continued his journey towards the hill top.

An hour of walking then enabled Harry to reach the top of the hill and from there he could see that it had been the lights from his village. Taking the time to sit and recover his breath, he then tried to work out where he had left his precious mini car prior to making his escape. Although there were no vehicles of any kind that he could see using the roads around the village. After picturing his escape route in his mind he remembered that there had been another hill top but this time with some trees on it. It had been from there that he had called the police for help. He must have left his mini somewhere towards the left of the village. This reasoning was only because to the right of the village there is a small stream and he hadn't come across that during his exploits!

He scoured the darkened skyline almost inch by inch for some sort of visual lead until the tops of trees began to shimmer in the half moonlight.

"That looks very much like the place if I am not mistaken," said Harry to himself and began heading towards it. He must have walked for at least another half an hour, climbing over fences and even a thorny hedge. Eventually he found that he was standing in the same field from where he had previously left his car. He knew that he had left it parked alongside a thick hedge that though, was when it had been daylight. So the only thing left to do was to begin the trek following the hedge until he came across his car. After trudging around the entire field he decided that those men who were chasing after him must have taken it.

The only thing left for him to do was to head back towards the village lights using the hedgerows for cover, that way if a vehicle should come along the road, he could dive into the hedge and hide.

As the lights grew brighter the nearer he became to the village, Harry's heart began to beat faster and faster. It was like a ghost town, there were no vehicles or people moving about, it just gave the place an unnatural and eerie feeling.

Then from nowhere a lorry suddenly came into view and Harry quickly threw himself behind a bush and watched which direction it was travelling in. Keeping out of sight using both the hedgerows and shrubbery, he managed to keep the lorry in sight, only because for some reason it was travelling very slowly. Eventually it came to a halt just in front of a set of large gates that were completely stretched across the entire road.

"I know this place," he thought to himself, "this is the place where they started shooting at me and my poor mini."

———————

Chapter six

Creeping along the ground on all fours, using the shadows and shrubbery as cover, Harry silently edged his way around the side of the lorry. He then managed to conceal himself within some large bushes that were positioned quite close to the gates. Slowly he parted the leaves to enable him to observe the gate entrance.

"Well, I wonder what's going to happen next?" thought Harry as he nervously crouched down behind the bushes.

Before too long, two armed guards appeared from out of the shadows, opened the gates and approached the lorry. It was only then that the driver and his mate, both climbed down from the cab, slamming the doors shut behind them. Then, after a brief discussion with the two guards they all walked casually towards the rear of the lorry. The vehicle looked like a seven tonne metal backed lorry that had twin opening doors to the rear. The two guards stood slightly back from the lorry as the driver and his mate opened up the rear doors.

As soon as the doors were opened, Harry saw what he thought was a dark shadowy figure spring from out of the rear of the lorry almost like an animal trying to escape capture. The driver and his mate were both taken by surprise and were knocked to the ground by the fleeing person.

  Having been there himself, Harry knew only too well the feelings of panic and terror that must be going around in that persons mind right now!

Try as he might to make a run for it, the escapee was soon overpowered by the two guards and brought down hard to the ground. This was the opportunity that Harry had been hoping for. In an instant and while the guards were distracted, he leapt to his feet and quickly but very quietly he made his way through the gates. Then once inside the compound, he disappeared back into the shadows of some other large bushes. From this new vantage point, he was now able to observe the tooing and froing movements that were constantly going on between the different buildings.

Over the next hour or so several lorry's arrived at the gates each had their rear compartments full of people who were then led away by armed guards. After observing these events for some time, it soon became apparent to Harry that everyone being brought here were under extreme duress and being herded just like they do with cattle through one particular door.

Watching from his hiding place, he could see what could only be described as terror and bewilderment on the faces of all of the men, women and children that were being forced by the men armed with guns into the building. From what he could see, the building concerned was a single story construction and looked as though it was a similar design to the ones that he had previously seen on industrial estates. They had always interested him by their almost self build construction look.

Now his concentration switched back to the lines of people funnelling into this one.

Some of the women were carrying their handbags but for the majority people, they only had with them what they were wearing. It was while he was watching such a movement he decided that it was going to be up to him and him alone, to try and save these people from whatever kind of fate now awaited them. The only answer he needed now though was how?

Before long, the lorry movement stopped and the outside gates were locked with only one guard left on duty. With the coast now clear, he moved himself so that he was situated along the side of the building that all of the people were now in. Soon, he managed to find a window that was at head height and carefully looked through it. To his amazement he found that he was actually looking down into what looked like a large hall.

That was when it dawned on him that the building that he was looking into must somehow have been built into the hillside. He by sheer luck had found a window that must be near to where the roof of the building was. Peering carefully through the glass, the sight that befell him left him feeling numb throughout his entire body.

For there, in the hall below him, he saw not a few, but hundreds of men, women and children and they were all huddling together in groups as if for safety. In the centre of the group it seemed that the adults had instinctively created a circle and corralled the children inside for their own safety. They in turn were then surrounded by the women and finally the outer circle was made up of the men and older boys. These were all facing in an outwards direction as if ready to defend the people behind them from any sort of attack, but from what or who?

After what seemed an eternity, a small group of people all dressed in long white coats entered through a side door situated at the far end of the hall. He watched as they stood behind a line of armed men and scanned the room full of people. They seemed to take pleasure in seeing all their terrified faces, it was only then, that the men turned and smiled menacingly to each other and nodded their heads. As Harry continued to watch the scene unfold below his stomach knotted up tight. Because, even from his position up high near the roof of the building, he could see the fear growing on the faces of the people that were now for some reason being held hostage!

Using his fingers, Harry managed to prize the window open just enough for him to hear what was being said.
  "You are all obviously wondering what is going on and also what is going to happen to all of you?" said one of the men in the small group in a sneering voice.
The people in the room below fell silent as they strained to listen to what was being said.

"Well, your small insignificant village has been chosen to be used in an experiment by the military. This experiment is to try out a new device that could be used against an enemy during a war scenario. Overnight a harmless gas was placed in and around your village and released. The only effects are that you are unable to see or read any words. In reality the words are still there but your ability to read them has been taken away from you.
Tonight the same military exercise will take place but this time the gas will reverse the symptoms so until then you will all have to remain here!"

"You can't do this, you just wait until the media hears about this!" shouted someone from the crowd.
That statement was greeted with some amusement by the men in white coats, who responded with, "Fortunately for us, you will not remember anything about this experiment in the morning as there is a slight amnesiac mixed within the antidote. You will all just think that

you have missed a day but please feel free to make notes, if you can remember how?" and began to laugh out loud.

This snide remark made some of the women and children burst into tears. A few of the men seeing how that unfeeling statement had upset their family members, made an angry move towards their captors.

"Nobody does this to our families and gets away with it," shouted some of the men as they lunged forward and began to fight with the armed guards.

Suddenly several shots rang out from other guards who were not involved with the skirmish. Harry had to quickly duck away from the window as he heard bullets ricochet off the roof beams close to him. By the time he plucked up enough courage to peer through the window again, all the fighting had finished. The result of the rebellion was several men receiving superficial head wounds, while a couple of the guards had black eyes.

Harry looked on as the women quickly rallied round, trying to bandage some of the men's cuts using hankies from their handbags. While all this was happening, the men dressed in white coats left the room along with their armed escort. A loud bang rang out through the room as the door to the large hall was slammed shut. Then the sound of heavy bolts being pushed into place could also be heard, this was obviously to ensure that the door would remain locked and the people kept secure inside!

Harry watched helplessly as some of the people frantically searched their pockets for anything to write with. Then one of them managed to find some paper and another person found an old bit of pencil in his coat pocket and passed it across to the man with the paper. Then Harry watched as the man tried time and time again to write something down on the scrap of paper. The men around him kept repeating what they wanted him to write down, but each time he tried to write, he found that he was incapable of putting anything down. One of the other men became impatient and snatched the paper and pencil from the man.

"What's the fucking hell's the matter with you, give it to me. If you can't do it then leave it to someone that can!" shouted the man as he attempted to put pencil to paper.

It was only at that point, amid his ranting, did he realise that even he had also forgotten how to write. Then the same look of horror was soon expressed on his face as of the other people around him, as one by one each of them realised that somehow they had all lost the ability to write anything down!

As Harry looked around the room it dawned on him that for the first time there were no armed guards left in the room at all. This gave him a sudden cold shiver down his spine and he wondered what was going to happen next? Harry feeling useless moved away from the window at leant against the wall of the building.

"Why is it, that evil scientist are all fucking snivelling little shits that always hide behind guns when creating hell on earth for ordinary people?" said Harry, as he racked his brain trying hard to collect his thoughts as to how he can help these people. He began to ponder about the events of the day and just what the outcome for him and all of the people in this building was going to be?

It was amid that very thought, when he was brought back to reality when he heard shouting coming from inside the building. At first he was unable to make out what was being said, so he went back to the window. He then pulled it open just enough for him to poke his head through to enable him to hear clearer what was being said. As he listened intently, from within the crowd came a shout that made Harry go weak at the knees.

The shouts were of "Gas, GAS!"
Harry watched as from the air vents inside the large room, a grey coloured mist was quickly spreading across the entire room. As the mist engulfed them, people grabbed hold of anyone who was standing next to them. Mothers and

fathers just had enough time to pull their children in close to them for safety, before they all began dropping down onto the floor. It was just as if they had all fallen asleep at the same time. Within seconds, everyone that was inside the room was collapsed on the floor.

Quickly pushing the window shut so that he would not be affected by the gas, he slowly slid down the wall. This sight had made Harry feel sick deep down in his stomach and with his head in his hands, a few tears began to roll down his cheeks. At first he began to tremble, then, soon his whole body began to shake violently and he began to wonder if he had just witnessed the mass murder of hundreds of men, women and children.

Knowing that there was nothing more that he could do to help those poor people, Harry stood up and began to edge his way along the side of the building. His intention was to head roughly in the direction that he had last seen those men in white coats and their guards go. With no plan in his head or any idea as to just what he alone could do against such overwhelming odds? He cautiously approached a doorway that he had previously come across situated in the side of the building.

Fate though, seemed to be somehow deciding things for him. Because from the other side of that very door, he suddenly heard a noise that sounded like clunk, it was similar to that of a bolt being slid open. With bated breath he watched as the door handle in front of him began to turn.

———————

Chapter seven

Now, Harry was not a violent person, in fact he was in real life, quite timid by nature. But after seeing what these heartless people had done to those defenceless people including young children. The blood in his body was now welling up and his temper was raging near to boiling point.

Seeing a large piece of wood lying on the ground, Harry reached down and snatched it up. Then keeping his back tight to the wall and with both of this hand's firmly gripping the piece of wood he waited for the door to open. Then as if it were in slow motion, a man dressed in an all in one outfit including a hood, came through the now open door. When he turned around to close the door behind him, Harry took the opportunity and drew the piece of wood back across his right shoulder and then swung it forward with all his might.

Thump!!

Harry hit the man across the back of the head with all of his strength with the piece of wood. The force of the blow to the back of the head resulted in a fine spray of blood spurting out of the wound covering Harry's face and arms. The man's head was then forced hard against the side of the building, resulting in a secondary injury. This time though it was to the front of his head, causing blood from his head wound to splatter against the wall. For a split second the man just stood there rocking as if in a daze, looking at him. This freaked Harry out and he hit him hard again but this time to the front of his head. The man although severely injured, appeared to just stand there staring at Harry. Then he dropped down with a heavy thud, letting out a low groan as his body made contact with the ground.

At first Harry felt great and jumped up and down with delight that he'd managed to overpower the enemy with comparative ease.

"That's for all those people that you've just killed, you bastard!" said Harry as he pointed down at the lifeless body on the ground.

It was shortly after saying that, the reality of his situation began to sink in when he realised that he might have in fact killed the man.

"Fucking hell, that's two people I could have killed in the past few hours," said Harry as he stared down at the blood stained body. "Well if I'm caught now, they would surely know that I'm responsible for this killing and probably be blamed for the death of the soldier earlier. They will probably kill me or at least make me disappear in retribution."

After quickly composing himself he peeped through the door to see if anyone else was around. Seeing no-one he quickly and quietly moved inside the door dragging the very heavy man's body in with him. Harry looked around and found a dirty old dustsheet on the floor and threw it over the man's body to hide it from any prying eyes. With a smug feeling inside, Harry turned to head along the corridor when a man's voice suddenly spoke to him from out from the darkness behind him.

"Stand still you bag of shit, I've got a gun in my hand and it is pointing directly at your fucking head!"
Harry froze, then, he turned slowly towards the sound of the voice only to be confronted by a man dressed in camouflage gear. Harry found that he was indeed looking down the barrel of a large hand gun and the bottom appeared to suddenly drop out of his world.

"What are you going to do with me?" asked Harry in a shaky voice.

"Well, I you attacked and probably killed that unarmed man for no reason. What had he ever done to you to deserve that? So I could shoot and kill you and say that I did it when I saw you attack him. So why don't you tell me why I shouldn't." came back the reply.

Harry watched nervously as the armed man, still with his gun aimed towards Harry slowly bent down and threw back the dirty sheet. "Now that wasn't a very nice thing to do to him, was it?" snapped the guard as he turned to face Harry but this time with even more hatred in his eyes. But before Harry was able to reply, another voice echoed from out of the darkness.

"No, and this is not going to be very nice for you either!"

The guard, hearing this began to turn around, at the same time, from out of the darkness Harry heard what sounded like a dull pop! Part in terror and part in curiosity Harry ducked and instinctively held his hands up in front of his face in a pathetic attempt to try to defend himself. Then through his open fingers he watched the guard suddenly lifted his hand up to his neck before dropping to the ground like a stone.

With the guard now lying motionless on the ground in front of him, Harry began to wonder what his fate was now going to be!

With his eyes now peering into the shadows, he watched with nervousness as a figure began to appear from out of the gloom. To his amazement he found himself looking into the face of a female but not just any female, this one was also very pretty and armed with a gun!

"Who are you?"asked Harry, "and was it really necessary to kill him?"

The female, who was about twenty years of age and was dressed in jeans and wearing a large thick jacket, looked briefly down at the guard on the floor then turned back to Harry and gave him a huge smile.

"Don't worry, he's not dead I only shot him using a tranquiliser gun. It should put him out for a few hours and boy oh boy, will he will have one hell of a headache when he wakes up but apart from that he'll be fine. Anyway, I've seen what you can get up to on your own."

"My names Harry Flynn," holding out his hand towards the young female.

"And my names Sue, Sue Chambers" extending her hand to shake his.

"Where did you appear from?" asked Harry intently.

"Well, I live with my parents on a farm a few miles from here. We were just getting ready to have our evening meal when armed men burst into our farmhouse and herded us all into a lorry. I only just had time to grab my dad's coat to put on," said Sue.

"When we arrived here and the doors were opened my dad tried to escape by jumping out. When I saw him being chased down the road I used the opportunity to slip out of the lorry and hid in the bushes just inside the gates. It was horrible to see my dad tackled to the ground like that but he's as strong as an ox, so I knew that he would be ok. From the bushes I saw you looking through the window and at first I thought that you might be associated with the armed men. Then when you hit that man over the head with such aggression I knew that you were obviously miffed about something so I decided to follow you."

"I'm very glad that you did but where on earth did you get hold of that tranquiliser gun?" asked Harry.
Sue smiled and replied, "Well that was just sheer luck really, because back at the farm when I grabbed a coat before being loaded into the lorry. I must have picked up my dad's coat and he must have been out on the farm using it. As usual put it back in his pocket instead of the gun safe where it is normally kept."
"Well I must say that I am extremely glad that he did and that you are a very good shot with it!" said Harry. "That shot to the neck especially from out of the darkness must have been very tricky?"

"Mmm, well to be truly honest, I was actually aiming at his back when I fired," sighed, Sue.
At first a look of horror came over Harry's face when he realised that he could have been shot

instead of the guard. He then saw the funny side of things and gave a big smile.

Harry then with a very sombre face moved towards Sue.

"Sue, I have to tell you something and you're not going to want to hear it," said Harry in a soft tone of voice.

"What do you mean?" replied Sue looking strangely at Harry.

Harry stood close to Sue and told her what he had seen down in the large hall. Sue at first just stared at him in disbelief, then tears began to tumble down her cheeks. Harry offered his arms towards her and they held on to each other for a while, both of them gleaning some comfort from another stranger's arms.

Sue then moved away from Harry and wiping the tears from her eyes said, "Right crying never solved anything as my dad used to say. Let's see what we can do to help rectify the situation shall we. I reckon that it's payback time?"

Harry, now inspired by Sue's outlook, smiled and nodded in agreement.

After dragging the guard to lie alongside the other man, Sue put the safety catch back on the gun then replaced it back in her jacket pocket. She then and helped Harry to cover both men over again with the dirty sheet and then the two of them proceeded cautiously along the corridor.

"Well how did it feel to kill someone?" asked Sue gingerly.

"Well to be honest with you, this will probably be the second person that I've killed today," said Harry quietly.

"Bloody hell, are you some sort of Rambo person or what!" replied Sue with a smile on her face.

Harry then quickly explained about the armed man by his old mini.

"This is very eerie place," said Sue quietly.

"We know that there are lots of people about but the silence is almost deafening!"

As they moved from one corridor to another from in the distance they suddenly could hear the sound of voices. So using the faint voices as a focal point they quietly headed towards them continuously looking around him.

Before long they found themselves standing outside the very room where the voices they had heard were coming from. Then by each pressing an ear hard against the door they both held their breath as they listened in on the conversation coming from within.

"Those people will remember nothing about what has happened here today," said one of the voices.

"Just think, we could do this kind experiment at anytime and virtually anywhere and nobody would be able to do a thing about it," laughed another, in a voice that was edged with no feeling or emotion.

"Yes, by now the guards will busy taking all of those sleeping people back to their own homes and by tomorrow they will remember nothing.

It means that the gas known only as (1120) is a complete success and even better we are the only ones that are aware about it. The best thing is that the antidote for the gas is only a high quantity of pure oxygen and that makes it very cheap to use," laughed the other voice.

That sound made Harry feel sick deep down in his stomach. He looked at Sue as she heard for the first time that her parents had not been killed in the large hall after all. This news however, made her go very weak at the knees. Seeing the look on Sues face, Harry instantly reached out and put his arms around her and just managed to whisk her up and cradle her before she could drop to the floor.

"At least now we know that none of those people including any of your family, actually lost their lives," he whispered in Sue's ear as he carried her further along the corridor and away from the door.

After trying several doors only to find they were all locked, Harry eventually found one that was open. He looked inside to make sure that it was empty then he helped Sue into the room and pulled up a chair for her to sit on. Over in the corner of the room was a small hand basin that would have been used to wash hands.

Below Harry found a cup and although it was a little dusty, basically all it required was a swill to make it usable.
While handing over the cup of cold water to Sue and watching her take small sips to moisten her mouth. The emotion of the past few hours swelled up inside him and he was unable to stem the flow of tears from tumbling down his face. Sue, seeing this stood up and went across to Harry and put her arm around his shoulders to comfort him.

  "I'm sorry," blurted out Harry, trying to control himself. "It's just hit me that I didn't actually witness the mass murder of all those men-women and children earlier."

Sue stooped down so that her face was looking directly into his and said softly, "That doesn't make you a weak person in my eyes, it only means that you really care and you shouldn't be ashamed of that!"

"No, it's not just that," said Harry. "It's that I've killed two people and they weren't responsible for killing anyone!" Soon Harry composed himself and had a good drink of water. "Sue, you told me earlier after you had just saved my life. That you lived on a farm and you were about to have your evening meal when all this blew up, is that right?" asked Harry.

"Yes, why do you ask?"

"Well you see I could owe you and your family a confession!" said Harry a little sheepishly.

"Why, what do you mean?" replied Sue inquisitively.

Harry then went on to tell her about his day, first at the train station, then his escape from armed guards and finally falling through the ground. Sue listened with eager ears up to the part when he told her that it could have been her farm that he had entered and eaten his full of food. It was at that point her face seemed to explode with laughter letting out a piercing shriek. When she realised what she had done she placed her hands over her mouth so as to stifle any other outcries. Moving quickly across the room to the door, Harry carefully opened it slowly and peeped outside. After listening for any approaching footsteps, of which there were none.

He noticed that not far along the corridor from where they were, was a flight of stairs that went upwards. Harry gestured to Sue to follow him out of the office and to the foot of the stairs. Then after a good look round, they made their way to the top of the stairs and had a good look around. There were only two rooms up there and both of them were empty apart from a few boxes and bits of old furniture. Sue while looking out of one of the windows suddenly called to Harry and ushered him to come over to where she was. When he reached her, Sue pointed towards the window and told for him to take a look outside.

Harry after wiping the pane of glass with his hands to get a clearer view, could just make out some lorry's parked under some lights, that were being loaded up with people. These people though, were not walking they were each being carried to the vehicles by one or more men and then man handled into the rear of each lorry. Eventually all of the vehicles must have been loaded and dispatched because once again the front gates were locked and guarded. An eerie silence fell on the building which was strange because even before the lorry movement there had little or no noise heard anywhere. Maybe it was the fact that they were the only other people there, apart from the men in white coats and the armed guards.

"I think that it's time that we too left this place and made our own escape," said Harry.
Sue looked around her then nodded her approval and they both descended back down the flight of stairs into the maze of corridors.

Standing at the base of the stairs Sue asked Harry, "Which way did we come from?"

"That's a good question," replied Harry looking for some sort of clue along each end of the corridor. "I've only just realised that every passageway looks the same."

"Look, if you were here on your own," asked Sue. "Which direction would you take?"

Harry again looked both ways then decided that he would go down the right hand side corridor. So with a shrug of the shoulders Sue turned and walked along with Harry. They hadn't travelled far when once again the sound of voices could be heard and this time they were travelling towards them.

With more than a slight panic in their bodies they each took a side of the corridor and tried every door handle that they came to looking for one that was unlocked. Eventually Sue gestured to Harry that she had found one. This was not a moment too soon because as soon as they had both entered the room and closed the door behind them. They heard the sound of guards moving along the corridor and they sounded as though they were checking the door handles to see if the rooms were still locked.

Harry gestured to Sue to stand to one side and he would try to hold the door handle tight hoping to give the impression that it was locked. So willing up all of his strength he grabbed the round door handle using both hands and gripped as tight as he could. The perspiration on Harry's face began to run down his forehead then off the tip of his nose and finally onto the floor. He listened to the guards talking to each other as they drew closer and closer by the second.
Then as the guards tried the door next to theirs, Harry, all of a sudden felt Sue push her hand in between his and using her finger tips turned the locking mechanism that was located within the centre of the door handle itself.
She then took hold of Harry's hands and removed them from the door handle just as the guard outside tried to turn it. With the guards voices fading into the distance Harry turned to

Sue and asked her, "How did you know how did you know how to do that?"

Sue looked at him and smiled then replied,

"That's easy I used to work in an office building similar to this in the city. The last one out at the end of the day had to put the lock on the door. Luckily for me it is the same type of door lock that was used in here."

Harry smiled back at Sue and moved to one side so that she could now unlock the door, they could now try to make their own escape from this place. As they moved along what seemed a never ending maze of corridors, finally, they found a door that led them to the outside perimeter of the building. Stepping through the door and out into the cool night air was so invigorating after being inside the building for so long.

Using the bushes as cover, they made their way towards the front gate. When they reached the gates to their dismay there were two armed guards patrolling back and forth. Harry also took note that even if the guards had not been there, because the gates were not only chained and padlocked but had what is called dannet wire along the top to prevent anyone climbing over it. Dannet wire is not like any wire that you might find around say, a farmer's field. This is wire that has small razor blade shaped pieces incorporated all along the wire and they are very, very sharp. With that avenue of escape now not an option, they decided to move back inside the building and hopefully come up with a plan of action.

Chapter eight

Using the same door to regain entrance to the building where they had previously left the guards lying under wraps, so to speak. They entered through the door very cautiously. Again they moved along the corridors until they found an empty room and took up refuge inside it.

"How are we going to make our escape from here?" asked Sue.

"Mmm, I'm not sure about that one!" replied Harry as he began to take a look around the room.

Sue watched as Harry, using the light from the corridor to illuminate the most of the room, made an inspection of some boxes that had been stacked on top of each other. In the first few boxes he only found reams of office paper. One of the other's had hundreds of disposable gloves inside.

Then inside the last door he came across a black coloured metal box with handles on each end. Quietly he undid the clips that were holding it shut, then, opened it up.

Harry suddenly let out a loud GASP because there in front of him stood two grey coloured canisters each marked with the numbers, (1120)! At first the sight of these grey objects made Harry's stomach knot up tight. Then slowly a plan began to etch itself in his brain and a wry smile came on his face for the first time today. Picking up the two canisters carefully, Harry made his way across the room to where Sue was sitting on a table.

"Look what I have found hidden in one of those boxes over there!" said Harry with a smug sound to his voice.

Sue looked at the two canisters in his hands and replied. "Well, what are they?"

"These," answered Harry. "Are containers of the gas that was used on all of the people that live in and around the village?
If you remember when we were both listening to those men through the door and they were talking about the gas that they had used. Well these two canisters have the same number printed on the side (1120) that they had been talking about."

"Fine, but what can we do with it?" asked Sue.
"Well I haven't thought it out yet but I believe that if we could manage to trap all or at least most of the people here inside that large hall. Then we could carry these containers around to that window that you saw me looking in to. We could then drop them both through it the opening and give the ones in the hall a taste of their own medicine! What do you think?"

At first Sue said nothing, then, she must have had an idea because in a flash her face lit up and a broad beaming smile stretched across her whole face.

"What we need is one of their radio's or walkie- talkies," said Sue jumping to her feet.

"We need to find a guard that is on his own and somehow relieve him of his radio,"

"Good idea," replied Harry, "but why would he hand over his radio to us?"

Sue looked at Harry then slid her hand inside her baggy coat and took out the tranquilizer gun. She then searched the other pockets and eventually cried out, yes!

Harry watched with much interest as she carefully took out a slim container, almost like a posh cigarette case, from out of one of the deep pockets of the dad's old coat.

"What is that?" asked Harry with interest.

"These are tranquilizer darts for use in the gun," replied Sue opening the case and loading a dart into the gun and priming it.

"What are those darts normally used for?" asked Harry.

"Mmm, I think they are for knocking out any unruly or aggressive animals on the farm," answered Sue making sure that the safety switch was in the on position.

"Could that dart knock out a bull?" asked Harry inquisitively.

"Oh, yes, it would go out like a light," smiled Sue, putting the gun back in her pocket.

"What would it do to a man if you shot him with it?" asked Harry.

"Why should I care, they had no feelings for all of the other people did they!" snapped back Sue.

Harry, realising that he was not going to win this argument decided to drop the subject and try along with Sue to come up with a plan of action.

"Right I have it," said Sue standing up. "What we will do is make our way back to the place where we saw the stairs and wait until a guard comes along."

"Great, what then?" said Harry, who still was looking at her in a confused state.

"Well, I'll sit on the stairs and look helpless," said Sue, "and when the guard comes up to talk to me you will shoot him with the dart gun!"

"Me! I've never shot a gun in my life!" spluttered Harry.

"Well now is the time to start," replied Sue.

"But just remember, I will be in a very vulnerable position out there so you must make the first shot counts."

Sue then removed the dart gun from her pocket and handed over to Harry. With trembling hands Harry took hold of the gun and for some reason decided to look down the barrel!

"Don't do that!" snapped Sue, "look, this is where you take off the safety catch prior to you firing the gun. Do you understand that?" she uttered with a huff in her voice.

Harry, feeling a bit of an idiot after realising what he had just done, nodded his head and placed the gun in his trouser pocket.

So with a sort of plan in their heads, they left the room and headed back towards where the stairs had been. On arrival at the stairs they looked for the nearest room for Harry to wait and hide in.

Unfortunately the nearest open room was some twenty yards away from the stairway.

"Remember, you must get as close as you can to the guard before firing the gun or the dart will not have the desired affect and knock him out." So while Sue took up her position sitting on the bottom couple of steps of the stairs, Harry practiced his approach from the office door to where Sue would be sitting on the stairs. Eventually after several attempts, they agreed on what the desired distance should be before Harry was to fire the gun. All they had to do now was to wait for someone to come along.

As Harry took up position in the side office, he watched Sue sitting on the stairs through the doorway. He, for the first time noticed how beautiful she was sitting on the stairs in her jeans and wearing an old baggy coat of her fathers. He seemed for some reason unable to take his eyes of her and was a little curious when he saw her take what looked like a scrap of paper from out of her dad's coat pocket. Then using something looked as though she was trying to write something on it!

What a shame he thought to himself, she obviously has not realised yet that she will not be able to write anything. She must, like me and all those people in the hall still be affected by the drug and be unable to see any words and hence not be able to write anything down!

Harry was just about to go along and explain that fact to her when the sound of someone could be heard in the corridor. By the sound of the voice it was a male and it sounded as though he was singing to himself. Harry pushed the door until it was almost closed and with one eye on Sue he carefully removed the dart gun from his trouser pocket.

As the guard approached a bend in the corridor he suddenly stopped and listened. Quietly he moved to the corner he was sure that he could hear someone crying, but who?

He poked his head slowly around the corner and was surprised when there in front of him sat on the bottom couple of steps of the stairs crying, was a young female.

It was obvious to him that she had no idea that he was there because her head was buried into her arms that in turn were resting on her knees.

"Who are you and what are you doing here?" asked the guard as he cautiously approached her. He had barely finished asking the question, when the young female began to cry out even louder.

Harry watched intently as the guard stood next to Sue and leant over so as if to talk to her. This was Harry's cue. He opened the office door and on tip toe moved along the corridor towards the guard with the dart gun pointing directly at the back of the guard. As soon as Harry reached the agreed point he half closed his eyes and pulled the trigger.

To his amazement nothing happened, he tried again and again with the same results. Sue who was looking at Harry through the corner of her eye realised what was wrong and lifted her face to look at the guard and muttered the word safety!

The guard looked into her eyes and replied, what do you mean safety, you are in no danger here. When Harry heard the words being repeated it was like a rock hitting him and using his thumb he moved the safety switch on the gun to red and then pulled the trigger.

POP!

The sound although not very loud seemed to reverberate along the corridor. Within a second of the gun going off, the guard heard it and began to turn towards Harry. As luck would have it, although Harry had been aiming at the guards back, he actually hit him in the behind! The guard just had enough time to let a cry of

"What the," before the drug took effect and he dropped to the floor with a loud thump!

"Phew, that was close," uttered Sue while standing up.

"You can tell me, if you hadn't thought to say the word safety, I dread to think where we would be now!" replied Harry with his hands still shaking.

Seeing the state he was in, Sue gently took the gun from his hand and after replacing the safety, put it back inside her coat. They then between them dragged the now desperately heavy guard into the office and began to search through his pockets. In his top tunic pocket they found a radio and Sue took hold of that.

"Oh damn," said Sue stamping on the floor.

"What's the matter?" asked Harry curiously.

"It's the bloody radio, it's busted," replied Sue tossing it into the corner of the room. "The guard must have fallen on it when he hit the floor!"

Harry shook his head when he heard that the radio was useless. He then bent down and picked up the guards gun and then asked Sue, "Do you think that we will need this?"

Sue looked up and shook her head, "No, if we were found with a real gun then someone could shoot us for real."

Harry nodded and hid the gun behind some boxes that were the other side of the room. Then after closing the door behind them they began to make their way back along the corridor. As they moved further along the corridor than they had been before. They suddenly approached a cross section where it looked as though it branched off into four corridors. They took their time and peered around each corner prior to moving out into the open. Three of the corridors were empty however, the fourth was not. In the distance, they could see that there was a guard positioned outside a door.

"I wonder what he's doing down there?" said Harry to Sue.

Sue took a peek and then gave a wry smile to Harry and nodded her head. "Do you think you could carry me down as far as that guard?"

Harry looked old fashioned at her, then took a second look at the distance down to the guard and replied, "Err, yes, I think so. Why do you ask?"

That was when Sue told Harry her cunning plan.

Chapter nine

"Please can you help me sir?" said Harry as he made his way along the corridor towards the guard carrying Sue.
The guard looked confused at first, when he heard a man's voice call out to him and saw someone coming towards him carrying a female very precariously in his arms.

"What the hell are you doing down here?" called the guard to Harry.

"Please sir, his woman suddenly collapsed and she appears to not to be breathing," replied Harry submissively, as he drew closer to the guard with the sound of panic in his voice. "Oh please will you help me. She's a lot heavier than she looks and I don't think I can hold her up for very much longer." As Harry started to half stumble just in front of where the guard was standing.

"Oh, hang on a minute and I'll give you a hand," replied the guard as he slung his weapon over his shoulder then moved towards Harry to give him some assistance.

When the guard reached out to try and take Sue from Harry's arms, Sue suddenly produced the gun from her coat pocket and pressed it against his chest and pulled the trigger.

Pop!

Almost instantly, the guard gave out a deep sigh just before he collapsed to the ground.

"Oh so I'm heavy am I?" said Sue as Harry lowered her feet to the ground.

"No, I didn't mean that, I was only trying to give a reason to the guard hoping that he might come closer to help me carry you, that's all!" said Harry trying hard to make up a viable defence.

"Mmm, ok if that's what you really meant," replied Sue with the tranquilizer gun still in her hand.

"No, honest," said Harry holding out his hands hoping to emphasize the meaning to Sue. Harry then watched as Sue replaced the gun in her coat pocket and a smile began to stretch across her face.

"You bastard!" said Harry when he saw her smile that enigmatic smile that he had come to like. "You were having me going all the time."

"Hey, a girl's got to have some fun you know!" replied Sue, as she reached down and picked up the guards radio. "Good, this one still works!"

"Right then, let's get back to where those canisters were kept and give them some payback, shall we?" said Harry.

Sue was just about to follow Harry when she suddenly stopped. "Harry, come here a minute!" said Sue in little more than a whisper.

Harry stopped and put his head on one side as if he was trying to listen for something. Then he said quietly," What's the matter?"

"I wonder what's hidden behind here that needs an armed guard standing outside to protect it?" said Sue with a puzzled look on her face.

"Who cares," replied Harry as he urged her to come with him. "One of his buddies could turn up at any moment and catch us if we don't get a move on."

Sue appeared to be totally oblivious to Harry's pleas and went over and straddled the unconscious guard and began to search through his pockets.

"What are you doing now?" asked Harry in despair as he watched her rifling through his pockets.

"I'm looking for the key to that door, that's what I'm doing," replied Sue sounding exasperated at all Harry's questions. "If you come and help me, then it will halve the time we need to be here won't it?"

Harry threw his arms into the air as he resigned himself to helping her search the guard.

"Here it is," said Sue all of a sudden as she produced some keys from out of the guard's tunic pocket. "Now, let's see what's hidden behind the door shall we?"

Harry watched closely as Sue tried some of the keys into the lock on the door. Eventually, one of them turned unlocking the door with a click. Cautiously she turned the door handle and pushed the door inwards just enough for her to poke her head around and take a look inside the room. Realising that the room was empty, apart from a few metal tins that were stacked up on top of a table, Sue gestured to Harry to come inside. Harry shrugged his shoulders in disbelief as he watched Sue disappear inside the room. Then instinctively, he grabbed hold of the sleeping guard's tunic and began dragging him along the floor and inside the room.

"This is stupid," said Harry as he heaped the guard into one of the corners. "If anyone comes down that corridor now, were both goner be really in the shit!"

"Oh shush," said Sue as she made her way across the room towards the metal boxes. "I wonder what's so important in these things that it needs to a guard outside."

Before Harry could reply, Sue had unclipped the two metal catches on the front of the one box and opening up the lid. Then after peeping inside the box she suddenly let out a deep sigh and sat on the top of the table almost in a state of shock.

"What is it, what have you found?" asked Harry when he saw the state that Sue was now in.

"Harry, come and take a look inside here and tell me what you see?" said Sue pointing towards the box.

Harry faltered for a second, wondering what she'd seen. Then curiosity got the better of him and he drew closer to the box. He gingerly made his way and stand alongside Sue, then looking into the box he saw wads of bank notes all bundled together with paper wraps. "Bloody hell, there must be thousands in there."

"Well if the other boxes all have the same inside, then there could be over a million pounds there in front of us," replied Su as she moved the one box to the side and began opening another.

Harry watched as the lid was raised revealing yet again wads of bank notes.

"Why would they have all this money just lying around?" asked Harry as he picked up one of the wads of notes and held them up to his ear and flicked through them with his thumb. "I've never been this close to so much money in my life!"

"Me neither," said Sue as she opened up the remaining boxes. "What worries me now is where it all came from and what do they intend to doing with it?"

"I think we should be more concerned about getting the hell out of here, never mind what they are doing with all this money," said Harry as he opened the door slightly and peeped out into the corridor making sure that the coast was still clear for them to escape.

"Why don't we take the money and hide it somewhere," said Sue all wide eyed.

"Oh, do you think that they're just going to let us carry all this money out of the front gate without any objection!" said Harry shaking his head in disbelief.

Sue fell quiet for a few seconds then, a huge smile suddenly appeared that seemed to stretch across her entire face. "What if they couldn't stop us getting away with the money?"

"And why would they do that?" asked Harry as he suddenly began to listen intently to her plan.

"Well, what if we could get them all into the main hall where they kept those people earlier and somehow lock all the doors so they couldn't get out. Then we could drop one of those canisters that you found upstairs, into the room through the upstairs window.

"But how are we going to get them into the hall in the first place?" asked Harry with his hands open and palm upwards.

She then reached into her coat pocket and took something out and held it up in front of Harry and said. "Remember this?"
Harry looked and immediately recognised the guard's radio that she was holding in her hand.

"I reckon if you were to make an announcement over this radio, telling everyone

118

to assemble in the main hall, nobody would question that instruction seeing as it was being transmitted over their own radio equipment," said Sue as she batted her eyes at Harry and gave him a big smile.

Harry thought for a second and then replied,
"Ok, if you wait here, I'll nip back upstairs and get hold of those canisters. You, in the meantime look for something to put the money in that will make it easier for us to move when we're ready."
Sue gave him a kiss on his cheek for good luck and watched him as he opened the door carefully to make sure that the coast was clear. Then after a brief look back to give Sue a smile, he stepped out the doorway closing it quietly behind him. Then he disappeared along the corridor towards the stairs, at first he walked along quite blasé and quite light hearted especially after receiving a kiss from Sue who he thought was lovely. Then reality hit home with a vengeance, when a man who was dressed in army camouflage

suddenly stepped through a doorway directly in front of him.

"Behind you," shouted a man's voice.
The man who by now was still halfway through the open door turned to his right to see who was calling out the warning. Luckily for Harry, this was in the opposite direction to where he was approaching from. Harry lunged at the man with all his might throwing his entire bodyweight into the middle of the man's back. This sudden strike propelled the man into the upright of the door making him hit his head hard against the door's metal hinge. Instinctively, the man raised his hands up his head and felt for any bleeding. This was when Harry hit him on the back of his head with both fists ramming his head once more into the hinge. This time, the man emitted a low groan as he slid down the door unconscious onto the floor.

Harry, his heart in his mouth and every limb of his body shaking with fright, put his head around the door to see if there was anyone else left inside. Too his amazement, the room he was looking into was the men's toilet and it was empty. He grabbed hold of the guard's tunic and began to drag him inside the loo and out of sight of the corridor. It was then that Harry had a brainwave of sorts. He proceeded to take the man's trousers off and put them on over his own. Then he struggled to relieve the man of his tunic top and put that on. The finishing touch was the dark coloured beret which he slapped on the top of his head, not really having a clue how it should be worn. Then before leaving the man, he removed his trouser belt and tied him up with it as tight as he could. Then, Harry did up the tunic buttons and stepped out confidently into the corridor and made his way to the stairs.

Minutes later, Harry was tapping on the door while carrying the two canisters and waiting for Sue to open it for him. When Sue first opened the door and saw someone standing there dressed in army uniform. She immediately reached into her coat pocket and took out her tranquilizer gun and took aim.

"No, don't shoot me, I'm Harry?"
Sue gave him a stern look before she recognised him and lowered the gun.

"Blimey, you were really going to shoot me then, weren't you?" said Harry as he put down the canisters on the floor.

"Of course," replied Sue indignantly. "It seems the more you use this gun, the easier and more fun it gets."

Once back inside the room, Sue handed the radio over to Harry. He nervously took it and looked at the various buttons that were on the top of the radio to see which ones did what.

"It's now or never!" he said to Sue as he took a deep breath then pressed down the button on the side of the two-way radio.

Crackle, crackle, went the radio, as he held it down.

"Will all guards and personnel convene in the large hall immediately no weapons required, crackle, that is all"

With caution they made their way once again to the window that would enable them to look down inside the great hall. Again, using his fingers Harry prised the window open so that they could have a better view. From their vantage point Harry and Sue watched as the guards all filed in, stood around talking to each other and having a smoke. When he believed that they were all in the hall, Harry, leaving Sue to keep watch, he moved around the side of the building and quietly wedged the doors shut using some iron bars and pieces of wood or anything in fact that he could find lying around on the floor. Then wasting no time he moved around to the other side of the building and was just in time to see some men wearing white coats and overalls entering the hall from another side door. Once again as soon as they had all entered the hall, Harry secured that door this time using the same bolts that they had previously used.

Then Harry with a smug smile on his face went back up to the window and gave a big smile and thumbs up to Sue and they then both went back to the window to watch.

"What's going on?" asked one of the white-coated men, "and who was it that gave instructions for us all to assemble in this hall?" Everyone looked at each other and shrugged their shoulders. Harry then after tapping Sue on her shoulder opened the window and called out,

"I'm the one that gave you all instructions to assemble here."

When the people in the hall heard Harry's voice, everyone stopped what they were doing, then turned and looked up towards the open window near the roof where Harry and Sue were now leaning through. There were clearly signs of disbelief on some of the people's faces when they saw the pair looking down at them.

"After what we've seen you do to all those innocent people tonight, we thought that maybe you might not find it so funny if you also were not able to read or write!"

They all watched in silence as Harry dropped some papers and magazines down onto the floor of the hall that he had found in one of the offices and stuffed under his arm.

Then, with all of their eyes now firmly fixed onto the two faces that were now looking down on them, Harry and Sue each took hold of one of the grey canisters of gas and held it through the window of the hall. Harry, although still unable to read any words had managed to prime it, just by following the drawing diagrams that were on the side of the containers. That was the time when someone in the hall must have recognised the markings on the grey canisters and shouted out, "Look out he's somehow managed to get hold of the experimental gas canisters!"

When the others heard this, panic set in and they all tried to open, the now locked doors. That was when Harry put a big grin on his face and the two of them released their hold on the gas canister dropping it down onto the floor of the hall. Everyone stopped as if frozen when the canister hit the ground.

"Let's drop the other one in there as well!" said Sue as she handed it over for Harry to prime.

"Are you sure we need to use both of them?" asked Harry.

Why not," replied Sue. "Anyway, what else are we going to do with it?"

Sue then took the primed canister from Harry before he had a chance to change his mind and tossed it through the open window. They then watched and waited to see what was happening next. At first nothing happened, then, there was a loud pop closely followed by another as the two canisters, each began to release their noxious contents.

The gas then began to pour out into and quickly covering the entire room and began to rise up into the air. Harry seeing this happen quickly slammed the window shut so that the gas could not affect them again. He and Sue then stood and watched through the closed window as everyone began to run around with panic now etched on their faces. Then, with a final few gasps, one by one, they all dropped motionless to the ground.

  "Right then, shall we get back to where the money is and see about getting it away from these people," said Sue with a big smile on her face.
Harry took another look through the window to make sure that they were all still fast asleep, then, followed Sue along the side on the building towards the doorway.

————————

Chapter ten

Back in the room where the boxes of money were stacked up, Harry looked around for something to help them to move such a weight. In the corner of the room, he discovered a sack truck and wheeled it alongside the table. Then Sue and Harry took hold of a handle each and proceeded to pile the boxes onto the sack truck. With all five boxes on the truck, Sue had to help Harry to tilt it back allowing him to wheel the truck out of the room.

The journey along the narrow corridors was ungainly to say the least. Time after time, Harry would crash the sack truck into wall jarring his wrists and body in the process. Each doorway that they came to, Harry would have to wait nervously, while Sue armed with her tranquilizer gun carefully opened the door and checked to see if the coast was clear. Then she would hold the door open wide, allowing Harry and the truck to pass through. Finally, they reached to outer door to the building; Harry knew that if there were any guards left awake, then, this would be the place that they would meet up with them.

Once again, Sue did her thing of opening up the door and looking outside for any sign of the guards.

"It looks all clear," said Sue quietly, as she held open the door while Harry and the money passed by her.

"Where do we go now?" asked Harry putting the sack truck down to rest his arms.

"I think I saw a Land Rover parked down there from out the upstairs window," said Sue as she made her way alongside the building to look for it.

Harry just shook his head and began to wonder what exactly he was getting himself into, when he heard the sound of a diesel engine start up.

Then from around the corner, two headlights emerged and headed straight for him.

"Who was driving the vehicle and were they friendly or not?" thought Harry, as he just stood there frozen, watching the vehicles lights getting nearer and nearer to him.

Soon the vehicle was pulling up alongside him and Sue stuck her head out of the side window.

"Come on Harry chop-chop; let's get those boxes into the back of the Land Rover and get the hell out of here before anyone see's us!" said Sue as she opened the car's door and went round to the rear of the car.

Soon the boxes along with their valuable contents were safely stacked into the rear of the Land Rover and the doors slammed shut.

"You drive Harry," said Sue.

"Where are we going to?" asked Harry sounding totally bewildered.

"Why don't you take us back to the farm where you ate all the food," replied Sue with a smile on her face.

"Oh your families place but wouldn't it be quicker if you were to drive. I mean, I'm not sure where it actually is from the road!" said Harry.

"Oh come on, I'm sure you could find it again. Anyway what would you rather do, shoot the gun or drive the car?" said Sue holding up the tranquilizer gun and showing it to Harry. Harry looked at the gun in Sue's hand and remembered his last near fatal experience with the gun. It was at that moment in time that he decided that driving was by far the safest option, as he turned the key and started the engine.

The diesel engine spluttered into life sounding like nuts and bolts that were being shaken in a tin can.

"Well if there are any guards left outside, then this noisy bastard should bring them to us and soon," said Harry as he drove slowly towards the front gates.

When they got within sight of the huge metal gates, Harry stopped the car and they both looked to see if there was any movement nearby.

"You wait here while I go and take a look around by the front gates," said Sue as she opened the passenger door and stepped out. "If the coast is clear, then I'll signal you to drive too me, ok!"

"What if the coast's not clear?" asked Harry tentatively.

"Then I'll be caught and then you'll just have to work out how to get out of here on your own, won't you!" replied Sue, as she closed the door and made her way towards the gates.

Harry watched her edged ever closer to the gates and nervously kept looking into the wing mirrors of the car to make sure that nobody was trying to creep up on him. Then, after what seemed like an age. He saw Sue waving her arms beckoning him to drive to her. Harry started the engine and drove the car towards where Sue was standing.

"Is everything ok?" he asked.

"Well, yes and no!" replied Sue with a huff.

"Why what's wrong now?" asked Harry, wondering what she was going to say next.

"Well, the good news is that there aren't any guards about, the bad news though is that the gates are still locked," replied Sue as she pulled hard at the padlock that was holding the chained gates in place.

"Do you think that we could break it open if we drove the car at the gates?" said Harry, not really knowing whether it would work or not.

Sue looked at the padlock and then at the Land Rover and gave Harry a huge smile. "D'you know something, I think you've found the answer to our problem."

Harry returned the smile and put the car into reverse and backed the car away from the gates. Then when he thought that there was enough distance for him to get up enough speed for the task in hand, he stopped. Sue then climbed back into the car and they both put on their seatbelts.

Harry then revved up the car's engine, put it in gear and let out the clutch. The car lurched forward and in between changing gears, Harry kept his foot firmly planted on the floor of the car.

As they got within a few feet of the gates, Sue covered her face with her arms while Harry gripped hole tightly to the steering wheel.

Bang, crash!
The Land Rover collided with the metal gates ripping one side pillar out of the ground and propelling both the gates out of their way. The sudden impact with the gates however, threw a bone crunching shudder throughout the Land Rover, making Harry bite down hard on the tip of his tongue.
Once out of the compound and out on the open road, Harry took a second to wipe some blood from his bleeding mouth, before flooring the accelerator and disappearing towards the darkness and relative safety.

———————

Chapter eleven

With the smashed gates to the compound, now a distant sight in their rear view mirror. Sue let out a whoop of delight at their escape from the madmen. This delight at their escape however appeared premature, when out from one of the side roads, another Land Rover with two armed guards sitting in the front, screeched out and quickly drew alongside of them.

"Pull over and stop!" shouted one of the armed men as he pointed his automatic weapon at Harry.

"Don't stop, keep driving," screamed Sue as she stretched her foot across in front of Harry and stamped down hard on the accelerator.

"Fucking hell woman what's come over you are you trying to kill us or what?" shouted Harry as he fought to gain control of his vehicle.

"Look, if you stop now and they discover that you've killed at least one of their comrades and stole all this money to boot. I think that killing us quickly would be a blessing in disguise, don't you?" replied Sue as she kept her right foot planted down hard.

"Ok ok, I understand what you're saying," said Harry feeling pissed off that she was still stamping down on his foot. "Now take your foot off mine before I turn the ignition off and we both get caught!"
Sue stared hard at Harry trying to work out whether he would stop or not, if she did as he asked. Then she removed her foot from Harry's but at the same time, took out her tranquilizer gun from her coat pocket.

"What do you think you're going to do with that thing?" said Harry not feeling too safe with guns now on either side of him.

"If they force us to stop, then I'll shoot one of them while you tackle the other," replied Sue as she loaded the chamber with a dart.

"You can go fuck yourself if you think I'm going to take on one of those men, especially when both of them are armed!" said Harry as the guard driving the other car turned into their car ramming it from the side.

Harry responded by accelerating and them turning into their car, pushing it hard towards the right hand side of the road and towards a lamp post. This action and the fact that a metal lamp post was quickly looming towards them, made the guard slam on his brakes narrowly missing making contact with the lamp post.

Harry glanced into his side mirror at the other car as it once again roared along the street after them.

"Oh hell, here they come again," said Harry as he tried hard to keep the car driving straight while keeping the trailing vehicle in sight.

Bang!

The rear window in the Land Rover shattered when one of the trailing guards opened fire at their vehicle. Luckily for them, the incoming bullet hit one of the metal boxes holding the money.

"Huh, who says having plenty of money behind doesn't matter," said Sue in a whimsical manner.

"Are you kidding me, those bastards are trying to shoot us and you think it's amusing!" said Harry as he noticed the other car approaching them once more.

"Hang on tight!" shouted Harry as he slammed his right foot down hard on the brake pedal. The Land Rover's wheels all locked and the tyres skidded on the tarmac road surface raising puffs of black smoke into the air. Their car hadn't come to a halt before the trailing vehicle skidded and crashed into the rear of them. This action managed to force the tow bar on Harry's vehicle into the radiator of the guards. A plume of hot steam rose from the crushed radiator as the hot water escaped from the engine onto the roadway, rendering it unusable.

Harry, not wanting to wait around to see his handy work, put his vehicle into gear and they roared off into the darkness of the countryside, leaving the two guards still slumped lifeless in their vehicle. After they had travelled for a couple of miles without any sign of them being tracked, Harry pulled the car over and he got out and took a look at the rear of the car to see what damage had been done. To his amazement, only the tow bar had been bent slightly in the collision. The rest of the car appeared to be unscathed.

Getting back into the vehicle after having a good stretch, Harry turned to Sue and asked,
"Where's your farm from here?"
Sue looked out through the windscreen and replied, "Blimey, after what's just happened and in the darkness, I'm feeling a little shaken up and I'm not really sure. Maybe if we keep going along this road we will see something that will help to remind me!"

For the next thirty or so minutes, the pair zigzagged along various lanes, until finally, Harry recognised where he was in relation to the farm. Now with a smile from Sue, they drove along the long winding dirt covered driveway that led them to her home.

"What will your folks think about us turning up like this at this unearthly hour of the morning," said Harry not wanting to upset her parents any more than necessary.

"Oh, I shouldn't worry about them waking, I reckon that whatever it was that they dosed them up with will keep them knocked out for hours yet!" replied Sue with a smile.

As they pulled up in front of the farmhouse, Sue told Harry to drive around to the barn at the rear of the house and they could unload the boxes of money and store them under the bales of hay. Harry nodded and thought that for once, she was making some sense and drove the car right up to the entrance to the barn. Then under the moonlight that was shining down through holes in the roof old tatty roof. Their way inside of the barn was now being lit up with a pebble dash lighting effect from the moons rays.

With the boxes now well hidden from view, Sue suggested that they go back to the farmhouse and get something to eat. This pleased Harry no end as he was starving and also was desperate to use the loo.

Inside the kitchen, Sue told Harry to put on the kettle while she went and made sure that her folks were safely tucked up in bed. Harry not wanting to push things reluctantly agreed but at the same time was still desperate for the loo. A few minutes later Sue reappeared looking happy and told Harry that her folks were in bed and both out for the count.

"Great," replied Harry with his legs almost crossed. "But I desperately need to use your loo, otherwise there's going to be a bloody big smelly pool on the floor very soon!"

"Ok, it's upstairs and the second door on your right. But try not to make too much noise and wake them up prematurely will you!" replied Sue as she stood to one side and allowed Harry to pass by her.

Harry stood at the bottom of the old wooden stairs and looked upwards into the darkness. He then looked at the light switch positioned on the wall and wondered if he should use it or not. Caution however got the better of him and with not wanting to wake anyone up, he decided not to turn on the light and climbed up the stairs. Silence though was not going to be easily achieved for Harry as every time he trod on a stair, it creaked and groaned under his weight, until he moved onto the next one. But then that in turn did exactly the same.

Soon he managed to reach the toilet without waking anyone and had a big look of relief when re-emerged feeling a lot lighter than when he had gone in. While in the bathroom, he had taken the opportunity to open the small window and take a look outside to see if there was any movement happening near to the farmhouse. He stared out into the pitch blackness and scanned the area for any lights but he saw nothing. So with that little piece of mind, he closed the window to and made his way to the door. Then standing on the wooden landing while doing up his trousers. Harry decided to take a peep into one of the rooms just out of interest. The first room he entered was empty apart from oddments of furniture that looked as though they'd been stacked in there for years by the covering of dust that was obvious even through the moonlight that was shining through the curtain less window.

The next door that he opened was virtually a mirror image of the first one and looked as though it was being used as a store room rather than a bedroom. With that, he quietly closed the door to and was just about to go back down stairs when a thought suddenly struck him. As he stood on the landing, Harry counted how many doors there were.

"That's odd," thought Harry as he counted them again. "There's only four doors up here, one is for the bathroom and two others are empty. If the parents sleep in the remaining room, then where does Sue sleep? Harry had to take a look inside the final room just to satisfy his curiosity. He turned the door handle and pushed the door ajar just enough to look inside the room. There, lying in bed were a man and woman and they appeared to be out for the count. He was just about to close the door to, when he thought that he saw something shining and he decided to take a closer look. Moving slowly and quietly, Harry approached the side of the bed and looked down on the couple sleeping. It was then that something shiny caught his eye again and he bent down for a closer look. This time however in the side of both their necks, was a dart which had obviously been fired from Sue's tranquilizer gun.

Instinctively, Harry felt the side of their necks looking for any sign of a pulse. To his horror, neither of them had one meaning that they were both dead. The one question remaining was, was their deaths caused by the darts or something else?

Harry began to feel very uneasy as he closed the bedroom door to again, was Sue a cold blooded killer and was he going to be next. Harry nipped back into the bathroom and flushed the toilet. Then he took a deep breath and started down the staircase that would lead him back to Sue in the kitchen.

———————

Chapter twelve

"Everything alright?" said Sue as Harry stepped back into the kitchen. "You seemed to take ages up there."

"Yes thanks, although I was desperate to go, I think after suppressing the urge for so long. When I actually had the chance to go it took a little persuading but finally all is now well.

"I've made a cuppa, so why don't you pour it while I go and freshen up a bit," said Sue as she disappeared out of the kitchen.

Harry watched her as she went towards the stairs and he wondered if he had got her all wrong. She didn't act like she had just killed two people; in fact she looked and acted as if she was feeling at ease with the whole scene.

He decided to take a quick look around while she was upstairs. He moved to stand in the doorway that lead to the hall and listened. From upstairs, Harry could hear the sound of running water and felt a little easier about taking a look in some of the other downstairs rooms. He edged his way along the dark hallway until he came to an old wooden door. Taking hold of the door knob, he turned it and slowly opened the door and peeped inside the room. He desperately wanted to switch on the light but didn't want to let Sue know that he was snooping about.

So once again, he could only pick out things via the rays of moonlight that was shining through the window. It was clear that this was the lounge as he would call it. There was an old tatty three piece suite, that had seen much better days and oddments of old dark brown furniture scattered about the room. In the far corner was what looked like an old style television that was covered in dust, it was obvious to Harry that this room was rarely used. On the wall however, were a few framed pictures that looked like snaps of the family. Harry took a quick look into the hallway and once again listened for the sound of running water. When he could still here

147

the water running, he entered the room and peered at the pictures. One of them resembled the two dead people upstairs that had been taken many years ago when they both had been in there thirty's. One of the other pictures showed them on holiday with a small boy. Harry assumed that it could have been their son by his age. After looking at the others, Harry returned to the kitchen and poured out two mugs of tea.

When Sue returned, Harry was sitting at the old farmhouse table with a mug of tea in one hand and a biscuit in the other.

"Hey, where's mine then?" said Sue as she spotted Harry eating.

"Oh please, help yourself," replied Harry with a smile. "You know where they're kept."
Sue turned around and made her way towards the old dresser and opened up the cupboard.

"Ok, where have they put them this time?"
Harry looked up and replied, "Oh, I found this one in the tin marked biscuits on the side of the dresser."
Sue turned and looked at the tin and then replied,

"You smart arse, you moved them didn't you?" As she closed the cupboard to, picked up the tin and brought it across to the table and sat down.

For a while they sat there drinking tea and filling their faces with biscuits. Then Harry put down his mug and asked Sue, "Well what happens now?"

"What do you mean by that?" replied Sue looking at Harry with her head on one side.

"Well, we managed to escape being captured by the guards and then there's all that money that we stashed in the barn, where do you think it all came from?" said Harry open handed.

"Who cares where it came from," replied Sue with wide eyes. "It's where it's going to that I'm interested in."

"And where's that?"

"Ah wouldn't you like to know?" said Sue all secretively.

"Well yes I would seeing as half of that money is mine!" said Harry who was by now staring at Sue with a curious expression on his face.

"Anyhow, we'll have to find out just how much money is out there, before we can split it up."

"Err, what's this I hear about splitting the money," said Sue as her facial expression suddenly began to change from being the nice defenceless woman, to a granite faced stare that made Harry feel very uneasy. "I can tell you right now, that there will be no splitting of the cash. Oh I might decide o give you some spending money if you help me move the boxes to a safer place. But you can forget any idea of getting hold of anymore."

"But you wouldn't have been able to get the money away from those men without my help," said Harry.

"That's true," replied Sue with a half smile.

"That's why I needed to get you on my side from the outset. When I saw you take out that man when he came through the door with that piece of wood. That was when I knew that you were the one to help me get the money out of the compound."

"Hey hang on a minute, are you telling me that you knew that the money was there all the time, even before we came across it?" said Harry sitting back in his chair looking very confused.

"Of course I did," replied Sue scornfully. "Did you really think I'd escaped of the back of that lorry the way I told you?"

"But what about your dad leaping out of the back of the lorry trying to escape then," asked Harry, trying to make some sense out of what Sue was saying?

Sue lowered her head and when she raised it again there was a beaming smile on her face that seemed to stretch from one side to the other.

"You men are so bloody gullible, show them a defenceless female that is in danger and give out the impression that there might be more in the offing if they were to help out. They will always come to her rescue, especially if they think that they have a chance of getting inside her knickers, even if they have never seen you before," said Sue with a titter in her voice. "The truth of the matter is that I was never in any danger, in fact you were the only one that was.

You see, I was part of this ploy to test out experimental warfare tools on unsuspecting members of the public. At first, these little experiments where all legitimate tests and were aimed at small communities like yours. The idea was that the Army would be able to control that size of population without too much problem. After the tests were completed, there would be no memory of the event and everyone would just believe that they'd missed a day, that's all. My job was to monitor how the gasses affected the people before and afterwards. All went well until one of the scientists decided to have some fun with one of the females while she was under the affect of the gas. I discovered that when the test was all over, the female had no recollection of the attack and therefore no official report was ever filed."

"So what you're saying is that a rape took place and because of the gas she never remembered it happening!" said Harry shaking his head in disgust.

"Mm, well there were more than one rape taking place at any one time, especially when they realised that there was going to be no repercussions against them for their actions.

I used to visit these places afterwards to monitor if there had been any unwanted fall out with regards to what had happened. But each time there was none. It was then that I decided to have some fun of my own. Every time we had an experiment arranged in a place that had a bank or jewellery store and while the others were should I say otherwise occupied. I would get hold of the manager of those premises and tell them that if they didn't open their safe's and give me what I wanted, then their wives and daughters would be raped over and over again until they did. Surprisingly enough, none of the men refused me and hence I accrued this stash of money and uncut diamonds," said Sue rolling her eyes with excitement.

"And were the wives and daughters then left alone and not attacked?" asked Harry.

"Who cares," replied Sue almost laughing at the thought. "Well I mean, even if they were raped, they wouldn't have remembered it in the morning would they. So with that in mind, everyone's a winner!"

Harry could listen to this horror story no more and made a lunge for Sue. She unfortunately was ready for this and moved out of range and aimed her tranquilizer gun at Harry.

"Look I really don't want kill you," said Sue as she pointed her gun directly at Harry.

"What do you mean kill? I thought that those darts were only supposed to make you go to sleep?" said Harry as he stared down the barrel of the gun.

"Well that's what they would normally do I suppose, but these are a special batch of darts that have been brewed up from my own concoction, if they hit you then unfortunately there's no coming back," said Sue as she put her finger on the trigger as if ready to fire.

Harry looked around for something to defend himself with but all he had close to him was his mug of tea and a few biscuits.

"It's a shame that it's come to this," said Sue.
"I was really beginning to like you, but hey, business is business I say!"
Harry at that moment threw the mug of tea and its contents into the air hitting the light overhead. The bulb exploded when the liquid made contact showering the entire area with powdered glass fragments. Immediately that happened, Harry dropped to the floor and out of the line of fire. He then scurried out of the kitchen and into the farmyard desperately looking for somewhere to hide.

Sue, on the other hand, was wiping the powdered glass from her face trying to keep it out of her eyes. "You bastard, I'll kill you for that," she screamed as she run out of the kitchen and into the farmyard after him. "Come on where are you Harry, I'm sorry for getting upset like that, let's have a chat and maybe we can come to some sort of arrangement as far as the money goes anyway!" she said in a softer tone of voice.

From behind an old tractor, Harry looked on as Sue walked to and fro looking for him, all the time with her now infamous gun. She might be talking to him in a soft voice, but her facial expression was very different matter. He knew that he had to try and get to the barn where the Land Rover was still parked up. Maybe if he could make it there, he could use it to make his escape away from this mad woman and get some help. Harry watched Sue's every movement. Every time she moved away from where he was hiding, he would take the opportunity to edge his way nearer to the barn. Finally he caught a glimpse of the vehicle and when he though the coast was clear enough, he broke cover and made a break for it. Harry ran a full pelt until he reached the driver's door. He snatched it open and looked inside the vehicle for the ignition keys.

"Where the fuck are they?" said Harry quietly
to himself.

"Are you looking for these?" said a female
voice from behind him.

Harry froze when he heard that voice, he knew
that he was a dead duck if she decided to pull the
trigger now. Slowly he turned around and raised
his hands in the air. Once he was facing Sue, he
could see that dangling in her free hand were the
ignition keys for the car.

"I had a feeling that you'd try this mode of
escape," said Sue still smiling, realising that she
now had the upper hand and was holding all the
cards in this particular game.

"What happens now?" asked Harry as he once
again looked down the barrel of the gun.

"Well I could still kill you, I haven't decided
whether to or not yet," replied Sue, who was this
time keeping her distance from Harry.

"What will the others think back at the
compound when they finally get free from the
hall and they realise that you've taken all the

money for yourself?" asked Harry trying to delay Sue from making any rash full decisions.

Sue gave out a loud chilling laugh, when she heard what Harry had to say.

"Oh dear Harry, I don't think you really understand what really happened back there do you?" said Sue shaking her head and once again smiling. "You see, remember when we were tossing the canister into the hall where everyone was standing!"

"Yes and it was so that they would become disorientated and confused like all the other people had been earlier on. It was also to enable us to escape from the compound with the cash!" said Harry.

"Ah yes, well do you also remember me wanting to toss the other canister in as well and I handed it to you to prime before I tossed it through the window," said Sue wide eyed.

"Yes, what about it?" asked Harry who was by now beginning to feel a little concerned.

"Well that second canister wasn't the same as the first one that we tossed into the hall," said Sue.

"But it had the same numbers on the side of the canister that the first one had," replied Harry who was by now wondering what he had been party too.

"Mm, yes I know, you see when you were out of the room, I switched the labelling on that canister so that it would look the same," said Sue.

"But there were only two of those canisters in the room, so where did the other one come from?" asked Harry sounding rather confused with everything.

"Ah the second one had been hidden previously in one of the metal boxes just as a precaution you understand," said Sue smugly.

"So I was able to switch it over and change the label while you were out of the room. The second one had cyanide gas inside and when it popped it's valve, it meant that every person that knew about me was in that room and my secret would die with them, and die they'd an agonising death too. The rest is all history so to speak!" said Sue who was looking very happy with herself.

"But why did you have to kill the farmer and his wife like that?" asked Harry trying to stall her. "I realised that they were not your parents or in fact any relation of yours, when you didn't know how to find the farm earlier."

"Oh who's a clever clogs then. Ah well you see, when I went up stairs when we first arrived, they were starting to come round from the induced sleep. I had to stop them from discovering me so I put them out of their misery, end of discussion," said Sue as she stepped back away from Harry and moved towards the rear of the vehicle. "Right then Harry, all that remains is for you to load all those boxes of money into the back of the car and then I'll be on my way to a very different life than the one I've had up to now."

Harry moved slowly across to where the boxes were hidden and began to move the straw away from them.

"What's going to happen to me once these are loaded into the vehicle then?" asked Harry without turning around.

"Well maybe I'll just let you go or maybe not, It'll all depend on how I feel when you've finished!" replied Sue as she kept her distance and the gun aimed directly at Harry.

Harry was carrying the last box to the car when he asked her again what was going to be his fate!

"Mm, I'm really sorry Harry, you're a nice man and all that but you know too much to allow you to live so I'm sorry but!"
Sue then stood in front of Harry raised the gun and aimed it at his head and then gave Harry a final smile before she placed her finger on the trigger.

Bang!

A bullet ripped through Sue's right shoulder as a secondary bullet shot the tranquilizer gun out of her hand.

———————

Chapter thirteen

Harry looked on as her body was rocked by the bullets striking her, then the blood began to run down Sue's body from her shoulder wound. The tranquilizer gun was lying on the floor well out of her reach. Sue looked at her wound and then glared across at Harry and said, "You shot me, how, the fuck did you manage to do that?"

Harry then pointed to his left and for the first time, Sue realised that they were not alone. Then from behind, Sue's arms were grabbed and forced unceremoniously behind her back, handcuffs were firmly affixed preventing her from taking any more action against Harry or anyone else.

"Where did all these people come from?" snapped Sue as she seethed the words out between clenched teeth.

"What, these chaps, oh they're with me," said Harry in a matter of fact manner. "You see, we, that is to say my government department have had you and you're colleagues under surveillance for some time. In fact it was the banking anomalies that first drew our attention to your little escapades. You see, when banks cannot account for lost money, somewhere like my department is brought in to assess just who had the opportunity to relieve that money from them without leaving any clue behind.

Then information was received about unauthorised covert experiments being used against general members of the public. We then tracked all yours and their movements to establish that it was only after such covert experiments had been made, were the loss of the money discovered. However, knowing this and proving it was another matter. We needed a confession on tape from someone that had inside information before the Crown Prosecutor would proceed with any arrest warrants.

You Miss Chambers have just completed the circle that will put you and all your colleagues behind bars for a very long time indeed!"

"How did they know where to find us, so far out in the country? And when did you know that they were there?" asked Sue who was still in a state of shock from being shot.

"Well to answer your first question, well remember those guards that tried to ram us as we tried to escape. Well when they pulled alongside our vehicle, I managed to drop the address of the farm into their car through the open window. Then when they crashed into the rear of us and we made our escape, they knew exactly where to find us.

As for the second part, I knew they were there when you were pointing your gun at me in the kitchen. You weren't aware of it but a red dot suddenly appeared on your forehead, from the laser sights of one of my marksmen, who was positioned outside the farmhouse. So from then on, I knew that my men were covering my back so to speak," replied Harry.

"Ok you've got me there but who have you got that will be able to confirm what I told you, as you saw for yourself, their all now dead!" said Sue almost ranting the words out to Harry.

"Ah well that's another thing that I didn't tell you about," replied Harry as his colleagues began pulling up in various types of transport.

"Those people that were in the hall when we dropped those canisters in are all still very much alive. Everyone, of those canisters had been swapped for a non lethal stun gas, just after we'd first located them. You see some of my team were working undercover as guards within the compound. So you see there are plenty of people that will be willing to testify against you, especially since they found out that you intended to kill them all."

"So if they're all alive, then what're you going to charge me with then, robbing a few banks?" said Sue indignantly.

"No, not just that," replied Harry. "There will be multiple charges of murder as well. Seeing as until now we were under the impression that you had been using those darts to drug people and render them unconscious. However, we now have it from your own testimony that you were using a lethal drug that you knew would cause death on impact. The two people in the farmhouse are a clear testament to that end.

You know something funny, the irony of all this is that because these experiments were undertaken covertly and without the relevant people being in the know. None of the people that took part in these experiments will ever see the inside of a court to give testament that it ever took place. Instead, you will all be held without charge, in a secret establishment of our choice for the purpose of interrogation. That way we can discover how these types of experiments could go on for so long without being detected!"

"Then what will happen to us?" asked Sue in an almost scorning attitude.
"Well in the end, when we believe that you've told us everything you know, we might then let

you go but that is very unlikely," replied Harry
with a light hearted quip to his voice.

Sue lowered her head and began to cry out in
agony and screamed out that her shoulder was
hurting.
"Can't you fucking supermen handcuff me in
the front and ease the pain on my injured
shoulder, I mean, I'm just a lone female among
all you men, what can I do now?"

Harry gave a wry smile and said, "Ok, you can
handcuff her in the front and you can treat her
wounds at the same time," said Harry.
With that, one of the men unlocked her
handcuffs and was in the proceed of reattaching
them in front of her, when she head butted him
in the face and made a lunge for the tranquilizer
gun that was still lying on the ground. This all
occurred in a split second, taking everyone by
surprise. Harry looked on emotionless, as Sue
reached the gun and for a second stared deep
into Harry's eyes.

"Tell me Harry, is that your real name?" asked Sue.

Harry held out his hands gesturing to his colleagues for them all to stand still, then he looked down at her and replied calmly, "It is today but tomorrow who knows?"

Then before anyone could stop her, she turned the gun towards her and with a last smile at Harry, pulled the trigger. The dart from the gun hit her in the chest, not far from her heart. Within seconds of the dart making contact with her body, she was dead.

Harry bent down to check the pulse in her neck for any sign of life but after a few seconds told his colleagues that she was dead.

"We now need to wrap this place up as though we've never been here. The farmer and his wife will just have to disappear without trace, again leaving no trail back to our department. What's happening to everyone that was captured at the compound?" asked Harry to one of his colleagues.

"Oh they're being held under wraps for shall we say further questioning, sir. Then their fate will be decided by powers much greater than us!"

"Right now have you had confirmation that all the people caught up in this mess have been returned to their homes safely, and that there is nothing left anywhere within the confines of the village that can be traced back to us?" said Harry in his authoritarian tone of voice.

"Every things been wrapped up as tight as a duck arse, sir."

"Oh, have you got that bloody pill that reverses this word blindness?" asked Harry.

"Here it is sir," replied one of the men handing him the tablet and a drink of water.

"Right then after you've put her body in the back of the van, we'll get fuck out of this place and back to the city for some good food and some well earned sleep, until the next time that is!" said Harry as he climbed into a car and sped off into the darkness.

The End

Made in the USA
Charleston, SC
18 August 2011